# TRUMPED UP!

## *America in Peril*

**John A. Russo**



MOVIE EMPORIUM, INC.
216 Euclid Avenue
Glassport, PA 15045

# TRUMPED UP!

## *America in Peril*

**John A. Russo**

*TRUMPED UP: A  disturbing or dangerous situation created by sham and fakery, such as the undermining and imperiling of a constitutional democracy by a president of the United States.*

*"As democracy is perfected, the office of president represents, more and more closely, the inner soul of the people.  On some great and glorious day the plain folks of the land will reach their heart's desire at last and the White House will be adorned by a downright moron."*

*-- H.L. Mencken*

## *NOVELS BY JOHN RUSSO*

NIGHT OF THE LIVING DEAD
RETURN OF THE LIVING DEAD
THE MAJORETTES
MIDNIGHT
LIMB TO LIMB
BLACK CAT
THE AWAKENING
INHUMAN
BLOODSISTERS
DAY CARE
LIVING THINGS
HELL'S CREATION
THE SANITY WARD
THE HUNGRY DEAD
DEALEY PLAZA


## *NONFICTION*

MAKING MOVIES
SCARE TACTICS
HOW TO MAKE EXCITING MONEY MAKING MOVIES
THE DEATH OF OUR DEMOCRACY


## *FEATURE MOVIES*

NIGHT OF THE LIVING DEAD
RETURN OF THE LIVING DEAD
MIDNIGHT
THE BOOBY HATCH
THE MAJORETTES
HEARTSTOPPER
THE MOB BOSS AND THE SOUL SINGER
MY UNCLE JOHN IS A ZOMBIE

# TRUMPED UP!

## America in Peril

**John A. Russo**

"Russia, if you're listening, I hope you're able to find the 30,000 emails that are missing, because I think our press will reward you mightily."

-- Donald J. Trump

"We have a fool for a president.  A malevolent fool."
-- retired Lt. Colonel Ralph Peters

This book is dedicated to Russ Streiner, a good friend and fellow adventurer in the world of movie making and the world of political, social and cultural endeavors.

# TABLE OF CONTENTS

# FOREWORD

## "...the republic for which it stands..."

What are the words that we will recite when the republic is no more?  Will we pledge allegiance to the Fascist Plutocracy of the United States?  Will we meekly succumb to the unbridled power of the upper one percent over the other ninety-nine percent of us?

When the Constitutional Convention adjourned in 1789, a skeptical woman demanded of Benjamin Franklin, "What have you *given* us, Sir?"

He said, "A republic, Madam.  *If* you can keep it."

Republics are hard to keep.  They often don't survive the ignorance, gullibility or sheer indifference of their own citizens.  And when they fail, they give credence to the sarcastic axiom that people get the kind of government they deserve.

We must constantly strive to protect and preserve the constitutional democracy that our Founding Fathers bequeathed to us, and we must prove ourselves worthy of it.

We are in danger of losing it.  It is being eroded from within.

We are a nation so divided that we fear ourselves almost as much as we fear others.  Our various ideologies clash hatefully with one another, and our social and political discourse is poisoned with anger, distrust and contempt.  We may be defeated by our own failings.

The outcome is up to us.  And future generations will either bless us or curse us for it.

# PART ONE

# MY POLITICAL CREDENTIALS

"We don't say that a man who takes no interest in politics minds his own business; we say that he has no business here at all."
-- Pericles

"A good nation can go wrong; it's a fact of history."
-- David Ignatius on MSNBC

"The given world dazzles with wonder, poetry and purpose.  The man-made world, on the other hand, is a perverse realm of ego and envy, where power-mad cynics make false idols of themselves and where the meek have no inheritance because they have gladly surrendered it to their idols."
-- Dean Koontz

CHAPTER ONE

*How I Became Political*

Many people know that I co-authored the classic horror movie *Night of the Living Dead* and went on to write, produce or direct many terror-suspense movies and novels. But beyond that, I have always been deeply concerned with political and cultural issues. I wrote a book called *The Death of Our Democracy: An American Horror Story*, and some of my essays in that book are incorporated herein.

I have worked on dozens of political campaigns and have written, produced or directed dozens of political TV spots and documentaries. These kinds of films do not always carry screen credits for those who have made them; instead they sing the praises of whoever is running for office.

Most of my political work has been for people running for local offices, such as mayor, councilman, judge or county executive. But a substantial part of it has also been for campaigns of statewide or national significance: for example, for Lenore Romney, Mitt Romney's mother, when she ran for the governorship of Michigan; for Albert Brewer when he ran against George

Wallace for the governorship of Alabama; and for George McGovern when he ran for president of the United States.

I didn't just write, produce, shoot or edit the documentaries or TV spots for them, I also consulted and advised them on campaign strategy.  I took part in the inner workings of their  campaigns -- the deliberations, the intricacies and the subtle maneuvers of getting them elected to public office.  Or trying to -- because some of them lost in spite of our best efforts.

Politics is the art of the possible.  It is the means by which we progress as a society, hopefully into a brighter future, "a more perfect union."  Some of my books and movies are attempts to aid in that process and shed light on social and cultural problems in a way that might influence people's attitudes and opinions and move them in a beneficial direction.

For instance, I recently wrote and co-directed a Civil War documentary, *Hope Deferred*, that has a strong political and cultural slant to it, showing how women and children, black and white, had to suffer through the bloody conflict, and how the problems we did not solve back in 1865 still haunt us to this day.

My biggest and possibly best novel, *Dealey Plaza*, has been called "The great American Murder novel."  It garnered twenty-two Four-Star and Five-Star Reviews on Amazon.  "As real and frightening as today's headlines," it explores America's catastrophic addiction to guns and violence through four turbulent decades in the lives of five iconic Americans.

My interests and involvements are far more varied and complex than many of my horror fans realize. I have always been deeply concerned about all that goes on in the world.  I am an avid student of history, the arts and the humanities. I believe that it is imperative to study how events of the past have shaped the present and might shape the future.  William Faulkner famously said that the past is not only not dead, it is not even past.  That's exactly why those who do not learn from the mistakes of the past are doomed to repeat them.

## My Youthful Awakening to Politics

When I was  in grade school and junior high school, I was transfixed by Senator Joseph McCarthy's televised witch hunt against "commies and pinkos" and Senator Estes Kefauver's Congressional hearings on organized crime.  I began to realize the dynamic importance of national politics and the strange and often disconcerting forces at work in our country.

My millworker father was a life-long Democrat and a fervent union organizer back when scabs and thugs were used to break strikes and beat up or even kill people who were trying to secure the right to collective bargaining.  He loved President Truman (Give 'em Hell Harry) and was against Dwight D. Eisenhower when he ran for president in 1952 against Adlai Stevenson.  My sentiments were the same, largely influenced by my father's staunch views, but I had strong opinions of my own, too.

I was terribly disappointed when Stevenson lost.  He seemed to me to be more intellectual than Eisenhower, and I resented that he was called "an egghead" -- the insulting label often stuck onto liberals and intellectuals back when "plain everyday people" called them "snooty" and laughed and applauded when, in the movies, anybody "too brainy" slipped on  a banana peel or fell on his face in a mud puddle.

Anybody who "read too much" had to be wary of being called a sissy.  Kids in school made fun of me because I got good grades and read a lot of books.  So I had to work really hard to prove that I could play sandlot baseball and football pretty well and wouldn't back down from a fist fight.

I went to West Virginia University on a partial scholarship, started out in electrical engineering, found that I hated it, and dropped out, transferring into the College of Education with a major in English and a minor in physical science.

Around that time, in the early sixties, I worked on my first political campaign, as a volunteer.  I wanted to help Robert Baird to become mayor of my home town, Clairton, Pennsylvania.  I was a friend of the Baird Family, primarily of Bob and Jane Baird, who at that time were only about 20 years old, but later were investors and extras in *Night of the Living Dead.*

With an older friend who was a Democratic committee man, I canvassed the street I lived on at the time, Farnsworth Avenue, and the surrounding neighborhood.  Our ward was won by Mr. Baird by only eight votes, but the narrow win in that part of the city helped him become mayor.  I got a thrill out of being on a winning team and was proud of my contribution.

I had found that being active in politics could carry all the excitement of a winning season in baseball or football.

## A Mock Primary Possibly Rigged for John F. Kennedy

At age 21, I was the chairman of a delegation to a mock primary at West Virginia University when Jack Kennedy ran for the Democratic nomination in 1960. This was trumpeted as an extremely important event, with vast implications for national politics back then, although by now it is largely forgotten. The Kennedy backers were saying that if Kennedy could win the WVU mock primary it would prove that he had the support of the educated people of a Protestant and Republican state. The news media picked up on that party line because millions of voters thought that a Roman Catholic should never be president because his main allegiance would be to the Pope.

I was not for Kennedy, I was for Stuart Symington. I also suspected that something fishy was going on, because even though West Virginia had a Republican governor, it was a unique circumstance, in that the state was still in most respects heavily Democratic. In other words, the portrayal of West Virginia as a Protestant, Republican state was partly "trumped up."

The way that the mock primary was set up, the fraternities, sororities and other campus organizations would represent the states, territories and commonwealths of the union. When I registered my delegation, I was given the state of New Jersey to represent, with eight electoral votes.

That night, we were to go to the student union which was already decorated with flags, bunting, and so forth and in all respects a perfect stand-in for the Democratic Convention Hall.

In the meantime, I got an off-the-cuff phone call from Stuart Symington's son, Stuart Symington, Jr. He said he was a member of the branch of Tau Kappa Epsilon (my fraternity) at Yale, and he'd like to have dinner at my fraternity house. We were totally flattered and excited about this.

But, to make a long story short, when he sat down to dinner with me and all my fraters, he realized that he had made a mistake -- he was a Deke, not a Teke. So we had a good laugh over that. But he was glad that our delegation had voted for his father.

We learned that the Democratic Party had turned out some very heavy-hitters for our Mock Primary. Bobby Kennedy was there representing his brother, Jack. And Hubert Humphrey, Lyndon Johnson and all the other Primary candidates were also represented by national political figures, just as Stuart Symington, Jr., was there as a surrogate for his father.

This was heady stuff for me, as young as I was. And to add to my excitement, the national media really made a big deal out of this event. All the major TV networks were there, plus most of the major newspaper and magazine reporters and columnists. The whole thing had the feel of a real national convention, not just an imitation.

When we took the first ballot, Kennedy got the most votes, but not enough to get over the fifty-percent hump required for nomination, so we went into a second ballot. And halfway through it, a law student came up to me and whispered, "This Mock Primary has been rigged by the Kennedy people."

"Oh come on! How?" I challenged.

"The registration committee is totally made up of Kennedy people.  What's the first question they asked you?"

"Who our fraternity had voted for."

"Then they told you what state you would represent, right?"

"Yeah."

"Well, that's how they did it.  I bet you're representing a small state.  How many votes does your delegation have?"

"Eight."

"Well, they tried to make sure that Kennedy would win on the first ballot, but there weren't enough delegations that voted for him, so they came up short.  That's why there needs to be this second ballot.  We're trying to get everybody to pile their votes onto someone else so we can stop Kennedy."

I noticed Stuart Symington getting a Coke from a machine, and I went over there and told him that I had found out that the election was rigged.  He asked me how, but I could tell from the look on his face that he wasn't interested.  And I thought right then that he was in on it.  And if *he* was, then so was every other candidate.  At least that's what I thought at that time.

It was my first really shocking revelation about politics and its manipulations.

The bad part about it was that in those days the girls on campus had a midnight curfew and weren't there for the second ballot.  Therefore their votes could not be changed.

We tried to stop Kennedy, but in the end he still had the most votes, and the national media made a big deal out of that in all the reporting afterwards, even though those reporters knew full well how we were trying to change the outcome and why. None of them -- not *Time*, not *Newsweek* or any of the others -- reported on the rigging of a West Virginia Mock Primary that was hyped up to be an event of national importance.

I was terribly disillusioned, and after that I had a sour taste in my mouth about the Kennedy presidency. However, looking back at it, I have come to respect his powerful positive effect on the nation, and I always did regret his passing. I believe that his assassination, plus the assassinations of Bobby Kennedy and Martin Luther King, set America off on a bitter and tragic path that we are still on. And that, by the way, is the overriding theme of my biggest and best novel, *Dealey Plaza.*

## Filmmaking Leads Me to Greater Involvement in Politics

My life took some dramatic turns over the next two decades, and I was plunged even deeper into politics, on a local, state and even national level. After I graduated from college, I taught school for a couple of years, served two years on active duty in the United States Army, then joined George A. Romero and Russ Streiner in a small movie production company, The Latent Image, in Pittsburgh.

We made dozens of TV spots, documentaries and educational films and won many awards for our work in the years prior to the making of our first feature movie, *Night of the Living Dead.* A large chunk of our business had to do with political campaigns, mostly local campaigns for people running for city, county and state offices, plus quite a few gubernatorial races in many parts of the country.

Sometimes we worked for Democrats, and sometimes for Republicans. We produced TV spots for Pete Flaherty, a candidate for mayor of Pittsburgh who was a decided underdog, and our spots helped him pull off an upset. We also made commercials for John Tabor when he ran for mayor, and he lost, even though his campaign managers loved the spots, and so did we. I'm proud of them even to this day. One of the best ones was called *John Tabor Turned on the Lights*, and it showed how his elegantly simple idea of lighting up the city's playgrounds and basketball courts gave kids something to do after dark and kept them off the streets and out of trouble.

Working on political campaigns was exciting to me and my partners at The Latent Image, George Romero and Russ Streiner. It got the juices flowing because there were immediate and tangible results. The elections were either won or lost. The outcomes, for better or for worse, were perfectly clear, not like wondering whether our TV campaigns for Pittsburgh Brewing Company or H.J. Heinz Company actually caused people to drink more Iron City beer or use more Heinz ketchup.

## A Dangerous Adventure: Albert Brewer vs. George Wallace

One of the most exciting and demanding things I've ever done is shooting, directing and editing a thirty-minute documentary and a series of eight TV spots for the governor of Alabama, Albert Brewer, when he ran against

George Wallace in 1970. Wallace was a staunch segregationist all through the worst of the Civil Rights struggle, and Brewer was in my opinion more enlightened. The state was split right down the middle. We were told we had to be careful when we were among Wallace supporters because, in the words of one of the ad agency guys, "Wallace's boys aren't known for being peaceful. They're known for having shotguns mounted in the windows of their pickups."

This was not a joke, it was a serious warning, because right around that time, three Civil Rights crusaders had been murdered by Ku Klux Klan nuts. We were advised not to go down there in vehicles advertising with their Pennsylvania license plates that we were Yankees, and to cut our long hair or wear short-haired wigs so we wouldn't look like carpet-bagging hippies.

We were working for a prominent Washington, D.C., campaign management agency, Matt Reese Associates, but that fact had to be kept top secret. So everything was funneled through a Montgomery, Alabama, advertising company.

As the cameraman and director I was in charge of a film crew consisting of me, a recent hire named Paul McCollough, Russ Streiner and Russ's brother Gary. We also hired Joe Unitas as an assistant cameraman and lighting supervisor. He had worked a few days in the same capacities on *Night of the Living Dead.*

We were to shoot a thirty-minute documentary and eight TV spots promoting Governor Brewer. In nine days, we covered 6,000 miles racing to and from place to place, one city and town after another, and a lot of the time I was hanging out of back of the governor's limousine with the top down, using my camera to grab useful footage while going ninety miles an hour in his motorcade. The people of Alabama were big on state's rights, a vestige of the Confederacy, and their governor was treated like a president.

I had to interview on film a host of celebrities, noted political figures and lesser lights that the ad agency had lined up to give testimonials for Governor Brewer; folks such as German rocket scientist Werner Von Braun, legendary football coach "Bear" Bryant, a state supreme court justice, as well as Brewer's pastor, and Brewer's sister, all of whom were quite personable and articulate. A highlight for me was when I got to film Johnny Cash at a huge auditorium in Montgomery, at the height of his fame, delivering a great plug for Brewer.

The upshot of all this was that when I got back to Pittsburgh, I edited all the footage into the aforesaid documentary and TV spots we were to provide, and when Brewer's campaign managers saw the finished documentary, they said that it was the best political documentary they had ever seen.

And we beat George Wallace in the primary election! Back when it was the common wisdom that nobody could ever beat George Wallace in Alabama!

But, again, none of the candidates had over fifty percent of the vote, so there had to be a runoff. And, to my great amazement, the ad agency down there pulled the TV campaign off the air -- and all because of some ancient political maxim that "when you're ahead, you let the other guy do the scrambling."

And, like our liaison at Matt Reese Associates later said, "nobody scrambles like George Wallace."  We heard that Wallace hired black guys to heckle him and cause disturbances at his own rallies, and also his backers spread gossip that Brewer's two lovely young daughters, one a co-ed at the University of Alabama, and one enrolled at Auburn, were both pregnant to black guys.

Wallace won the runoff.

It turned out that this campaign that I had a key part in, back in 1970, was in many ways almost a mirror image of the campaign for the senate of Alabama in 2018 that was of extraordinary national significance.  Republican candidate Roy S. Moore was accused of sexual abuse and child molestation while running against Democrat Doug Jones, who had prosecuted and convicted the men responsible for a church bombing years ago in Montgomery that had killed three little black girls.

I was watching MSNBC one night when an elderly newspaper reporter elaborated upon the ironic similarities between Wallace versus Brewer in 1970 and Jones versus Moore in 2018.  I almost wanted to phone in and let everybody know that I had been closely involved in the decades-earlier campaign.  As a matter of fact, I had already been keenly aware of the parallels.

In 2018 the state was once again split down the middle between the candidate that I considered disreputable, Roy S. Moore, and the one that I felt was more enlightened, Doug Jones. Writing in *The New York Times*, Alexander Burns and Jonathan Martin said, "Mr. Jones's victory could have significant consequences on the national level, snarling Republicans' agenda in Washington and opening, for the first time, a realistic but still difficult path for Democrats to capture the Senate next year.  It amounted to a stinging snub of President Trump, who broke with much of his party and fully embraced Mr. Moore's candidacy, seeking to rally support for him in the closing days of the campaign."

The article went on to quote Jones, who said, "For once Alabama has declined to take the wrong fork at a political crossroads.  We have shown the country the way that we can be unified.  This entire race has been about dignity and respect.  This campaign has been about the rule of law."

## Lenore Romney's Trumped-up Campaign

While I was working on behalf of Governor Brewer in Alabama, George Romero was shooting and directing a documentary promoting Lenore Romney, Mitt Romney's mother, who was the Republican candidate for governor of Michigan.  Her husband George, who had served two terms in a row, was now ineligible to serve again, so his wife had been tapped to run in his place.

George Romero was still editing the documentary a few weeks later, so I was delegated to take a crew to Michigan to film the TV spots.  I used the same crew who had been with me in Alabama.

The Pittsburgh ad agency who had hired us was all psyched up, absolutely certain that Lenore was bound to win because of the famous Romney name.  Their concept for the TV commercials was that they would put Lenore on a street corner and she would answer questions from passersby on any political issue they wanted to ask her about.  I would have the camera on a shoulder pod, not a static tripod, the whole time, so I would have complete freedom of movement to capture all the interplay.  When the footage came back from our lab in Pittsburgh, the ad agency people would have all the voice takes transcribed and would then pick out choice segments to comprise six hard-hitting finished commercials.

Unfortunately, they had told me adamantly, in no uncertain terms, that I was not to get any cut-away shots; I was always to remain focused on Lenore so that viewers would know for sure that none of her answers to voters' questions had been tampered with.  I warned them that this would severely hamper the editing process and the timing of the spots for TV purposes, but they insisted that they were not worried about that.  And so, with great misgivings, I did as I was told.

However, during the filming I became convinced that Lenore Romney had nothing going for her but the Romney name.  She did not come off either articulate or knowledgeable.  In my estimation, voters would see right through her and she would lose the election.

On the plus side, I charmed the ad-agency people and they told George Romero and Russ Streiner how much they loved working with me.  But their good feelings toward me were not destined to last.

Instead of sticking to their (bad) plan of not putting any cuts in the TV spots, they proceeded to mark up the transcripts, putting ad hoc editing scripts together, timed to their own reading of the sentences and phrases, by means of a stopwatch.

Of course, they did not necessarily read at the same pace as Lenore Romney spoke, so when I put the clips together according to their instructions, each spot was six or eight seconds over the 60-second limit.

Now they hated me and blamed me for everything that went wrong.  They said it was my fault that Lenore's TV campaign was in jeopardy.  Then they butchered the raw footage even more, and ended up with a bunch of lousy television ads.

Meantime, George Romero finished editing the documentary, entitled *Lenore*, and it was an empty, glossy puff piece, totally phony.  This was not George's fault.  He followed their orders, the same as I did.  And the critics and the pundits lambasted not only the candidate but also "the image makers who tried to put one over on the electorate."

Of course I was right all along.  She lost the election.  And the ad agency people expressed wonderment that I had called the shot correctly and they had not, when they were supposed to be the experts on image building and I was only a cameraman.

## Gossip about Chappaquiddick

By coincidence, my wife Mary Lou and I were on our honeymoon in Martha's Vineyard in 1969 and were staying at a lovely resort hotel not far from the Kennedy compound in Edgartown.  So we passed by it almost every day when we went for walks or for dinner.

Also, when we walked from our room to the seashore, we would pass horses grazing in tall grass as we made our way down to the beach, where there was a picturesque lighthouse and eddy.  And it was the location where a few years later the scene from *Jaws* was filmed of hordes of panicked people who think they're running from a giant shark.  I mention this as a charming detail.

A perhaps less charming detail is that the same day that we were on an ocean-going ferry ship, leaving Martha's Vineyard, Ted Kennedy was apparently swimming away from the car he had driven off of a bridge, drowning Mary Jo Kopechne.

This of course was a huge scandal and a huge tragedy.  And around that time, I heard a story about what purportedly happened "for real" from a fraternity brother that I was talking to at a party during Homecoming at my alma mater, West Virginia University.

His first name was Al, and I might as well leave his last name out of it.  But he told me he had been at a party at the governor of West Virginia's State House, and it had been attended by some of the Kennedy people who had also been at the party in Chappaquiddick.

He said, "They told me that Ted Kennedy left the party with another woman, not Mary Jo Kopechne, and she was asleep in the backseat of the car and it was dark and they didn't see her.  It was only when they found Mary Jo's purse still at the cabin that they realized she was missing.  Ted and the other woman got out of the car and made it to safety without realizing there was another person in the backseat."

I don't know if this anecdote is fact or fiction.  But at the time I thought it made more sense than some of the other stuff that was being tossed around.  And it rang true that if Mary Jo didn't know she was leaving the party, but instead went outside, got into an unlocked vehicle and passed out, she would not have taken her purse with her. It's a tidy explanation for the tragedy that tends to exonerate Ted Kennedy.

But I don't know whether or not it's true.

CHAPTER TWO

*A Campaign Analysis*

Just to give you an idea of the scope of my work on some of the political campaigns I have already mentioned, this chapter contains an analysis I wrote back in the 1970's for Tom Foerster and Leonard Staisey, Democrats who were running for reelection as county commissioners. It doesn't just deal with local factors pertaining to the task of getting them elected, it also puts forth an overview of voter attitudes both locally and nationally that I felt we all needed to understand in order to solve our particular problems in building a winning campaign.

This campaign analysis is over thirty years old, and yet the points it makes remain valid even now. Staisey and Foerster believed that they had a credibility problem, and I pointed out how it could be solved, and the credibility issue remains an important one still, for almost every politician.

To me it is quite striking that this analysis starts out by focusing on the problem of getting people to actually go to the polls. Nothing has apparently changed, not only in that regard but in most of the matters that we were obliged to deal with back then.

## THE STAISEY-FOERSTER CAMPAIGN
**Viewpoints and Perspectives**

People nowadays, especially young people, are not easily motivated to go to the polls and vote.  Often when they do vote they do it more from an ingrained sense of duty than from any feeling that their ballot has any real effect or meaning.

Many people feel that when they vote for one politician over another they are simply choosing the lesser of two evils.  Elections happen now and then, and the names of the men in office change or stay the same, and the potholes remain in the roads and the traffic gets worse and wars go on and on and the youth stay alienated and the drug problem remains with us and nobody really knows how to solve anything and everyone is afraid to walk the streets at night.

People who  write books like *Future Shock* and *The Passing of the Modern Age* and *The Greening of America* have been very perceptive in documenting and describing the vast number of sociological ills which afflict modern society and which have produced a feeling of despair, futility and aimlessness in vast numbers of our citizens.

It has been shown time and again that large numbers of voters will vote for the man who promises a change, no matter how empty and hollow that promise may be.  This is because of the vague feeling that many have that things are so terrible right now that  any sort of change might bring an improvement.  Time and again people vote for a supposed change, only to find out that the only thing that changes is the list of names on the public payroll.

It has also been proven that large numbers of voters will cast their ballots for a candidate who has a quantity of personal magnetism, in other words that elusive quality, real or imagined or manufactured, that we have labeled "charisma." Certain of our public figures seem to have a charisma and they command the attention of the voting public. Ted Kennedy, Gene McCarthy, Spiro Agnew, each have their own brand of charisma, which is worth a great deal in the public marketplace.

So what does this mean to us as architects of a campaign? How can we use our understanding of people and the way people react to do something constructive for them and for ourselves? How can we motivate people to to believe once more that their ballot means something; that it makes sense to get out and vote for a man who is doing a good job; that the right people in public office can do something to improve the lot of each and every one of us?

Fortunately for us, there is a third factor which is often responsible for causing large numbers of people to cast their votes. That factor is, simply, *credibility*. It means that people will vote for a person who thinks, who reasons, who has strong, logical personal convictions and not prejudices, who has the humility to admit that he does not always know all the answers but is willing to explore and learn and discover the kind of understanding that leads to solutions.

If a candidate can inspire in the voting public the notion that he *is* the kind of man described above, he will get elected; and what's more, he'll deserve it.

We have, in our candidates and in their public record, the raw material to base our campaign on sincerity, on the evidence of the fruitful results of hard, intelligent work, and on the credibility of Leonard Staisey and Tom Foerster as county commissioners who have the necessary insights to do something good for Allegheny County.

We have credible candidates. The only reason that a credibility problem exists is because past campaigns have not succeeded in communicating their credibility to the public.

Now, credibility is a difficult thing to get across in thirty seconds, or sixty seconds, the length of a radio or television commercial. Commercials are best suited to communicating simple basic ideas about what a candidate has done or what he plans to do or how he feels about specific issues. In the primary campaign our radio and television spots were designed to do just that, and they succeeded well enough to help Staisey and Foerster get the nomination.

But the thing that was missing from the primary campaign, the thing that could have widened the margin of victory, is the overall *believability* of the candidates that can be communicated in a documentary film. In such a film, the viewer gets to experience more of the thinking that has gone into the candidate's decisions, to feel more of the personal touch behind the everyday job of being a county commissioner, and to develop a feeling of confidence that the right men are doing the job, with foresight and intelligence.

The documentary film will succeed in building the right confidence in the commissioners, and the radio and TV spots will home in on specific points to prove that the confidence of the public has not been misplaced.

To produce a documentary film that will answer the needs of the campaign, it will be necessary to film Mr. Staisey and Mr. Foerster in informal interview situations, in a relaxed and congenial atmosphere, designed to elicit the kinds of responses and the off-handed conversational feeling that will interest and inform the public. It will also be necessary to do a lot of filming which shows the commissioners doing their jobs and interacting with the public, in situations both formal and informal. We need to get across to all the voters the feeling that Mr. Staisey and Mr. Foerster have a genuine desire to deal with human problems in a human way, to find out what people need and what they believe, and how they feel their needs can best be served by the Commissioners of Allegheny County.

There will only be an outline script for the documentary at first. It will take shape as filming progresses. Then the best material will be selected, embellished with narration where necessary, and edited to a finished product. It is the best way to produce a documentary when you are after a warm, naturalistic flavor. It allows maximum freedom to do the best job of bringing out important aspects of the candidates' personalities which the public often does not get to experience during the fever pitch of a political campaign.

Some of the radio and TV spots will be written in advance and produced in accordance with a detailed script. Others may be lifted from good material that comes our way during the filming of the documentary. The purpose of the commercials is to supplement the documentary and reinforce points that can be dealt with in the space of thirty or sixty seconds.

For instance:

The documentary film shows people that Leonard Staisey and Tom Foerster are likable, logical men with a deep understanding of human problems.  Then a TV commercial on pollution control adds to the favorable impression already established by showing how the two Democratic commissioners have brought their logic and understanding to bear on this vital, specific issue.

By carefully designing all the TV and radio spots to reinforce the broad, overall campaign concept established by the documentary, we should be able to solve our apparent credibility problem and win the election for Staisey-Foerster.

NOTE:  They did win that election.

ALSO NOTE:  The essay you have just read, written over thirty years ago, makes the point that "time and again...large numbers of voters will vote for the man who promises a change, no matter how empty and hollow that promise may be."

You can readily guess the name of the president I think of when I re-read that long-ago sentence.

AND:  If you have an interest in writing campaign scripts, in the next chapter you may read the script that I wrote for the Staisey-Foerster documentary.

# CHAPTER THREE

*A Campaign Script*

OPEN disarmingly on a montage of impressive, dynamic scenes with naturalistic SFX (perhaps heightened a little) of aircraft landing, taking off and looking beautiful...at Pittsburgh International Airport.

As a plane wheels toward camera in extreme close-up with sunlight glinting off its cockpit, CUT TO:

Interview situation with a hard-hat construction worker on the site of construction at the airport with the impressive massive construction in the background. SFX of work taking place.

Still disarming the viewer, the interview comes off like something that might be seen on a TV news show.

The construction worker who is being interviewed must be rugged, masculine, enthusiastic about his job and the work in progress. Interviewer leads into questions and answers that point up the magnitude of the work being accomplished and the benefits for Pittsburgh and Allegheny County.

Final question, possibly and hopefully: Do you know who is responsible for seeing to it that progress is made for our county in projects like this one you're working on here?

Answer: Oh, yeah, I think that's the work of the county commissioners, Leonard Staisey and Tom Foerster.

TILT UP for great shot of girders and concrete against the sky.

FADE IN SUPER: STAISEY-FOERSTER, THE BUILDERS.

Hold the super and the scene for sufficient reading time, then fade to black.

FADE UP QUICKLY on scene of Leonard Staisey and Tom Foerster at the site of still more construction work in progress, probably at one of the community colleges.

NARRATOR says words like the following: Leonard Staisey and Tom Foerster *are* the builders. They've been hard at work, helping Allegheny County to grow. In education, in rapid transit and in pollution control Staisey and Foerster have been the leaders, pointing the way toward improving the quality of life for all our citizens..."

As NARRATOR talks, go to shots illustrating all the above things that he is pointing out. And culminate the montage at Allegheny Campus of the Community College where an interview is in progress with a black student who says very good things about how the Community College program has made it possible for him to get an education which he could not otherwise afford.  End this section on a happy campus scene showing many, many students entering the class buildings, taking advantage of the opportunity that has been provided.

Leonard Staisey's voice comes in, saying personable and interesting things about his reasons for taking an active interest in providing the opportunity for higher education for all the people of Allegheny County.  He might talk a little about the difficulty in getting the program started, how he had to secure the funding over the objections of certain kinds of short-sighted opposition.  As he talks, we dissolve to scenes which illustrate his points.

CUT TO: Tom Foerster riding in a jeep, inspecting an eroded area or something similar.

STAISEY continues to talk, pointing out how his and Tom's interest in higher education, in pollution control, etc., is an outgrowth of the feeling that life can only be made worthwhile if we improve the *quality* of life for *all* the people.

As we see scenes of FOERSTER on the job, testing streams, inspecting timber, and so forth, STAISEY'S VOICE will point out for us the sincerity and value of Tom's lifelong work in ecology, long before it became fashionable.

Then FOERSTER'S VOICE comes in, over scenes of the beauty of our county parks, as he talks about his own personal philosophy and the problems he has faced in carrying on the fight against polluters, in working with GASP, and in preserving the natural beauty of our surroundings.  Foerster will be on-camera for part of this rap, but for the beginning and conclusion his voice will ride over scenes which illustrate his main points.

CUT to Staisey and Foerster together, in some kind of interesting situation.  A discussion with college students or other young people might be good, or a sort of cracker-barrel session at a union hall.

Objective is to bring the candidates *together* finally, in this part of the film, to show them interacting well with each other informally.  Whatever this situation is, it should show people also reacting well to Staisey and Foerster.  It would help to have good cutaways of people laughing at a witty remark made by one of the candidates or responding warmly to a handshake or a friendly jibe.

The union hall situation has its appeal, either here or in some other part of the film, because of the warmth and rugged empathy which should rub off on the candidates in interaction with steel workers or other hard-working hard-drinking guys.

The NARRATOR at this point should  segue in as we go to a montage of scenes taken at rallies, picnics, hospitals, clinics, in other words at various social occasions where Staisey and Foerster actually get out and meet the people.

NARRATOR:  To serve the needs of the people it is necessary to get out and *meet* the people -- to talk with them, no holds barred -- in an honest attempt to discover how to do a big important job.  Tom Foerster and Leonard

Staisey have never been the kind of men who are content to do their job from such a great distance that they lose touch with the people.  They get out and learn; they get out and work at doing their job.  They want to know what's happening, first-hand.  Then they apply their knowledge to solve problems.

CUT TO Foerster, who is saying things which emphasize the points just made by the narrator, such as:

FOERSTER:  It's not all fun, by any means.  We have to find out what makes people tick.  We want to do a good job, one that has meaning.  People notice us when we're out talking to them, trying to discover how they want *us* to do the job for *them*.  They don't see the hours Leonard and I put in at a desk with nobody around but us and a mountain of paper...

Use FOERSTER'S VOICE over scenes of either Staisey alone in the office, laboring over paperwork or using his note-taking machine (that he uses because he is blind).  Or else use a lip-sync scene of Tom and Leonard working together and bouncing ideas off of each other, in the solitude of a late evening when everyone else has gone home for the day.

The idea of using each candidate's voice to highlight on-the-scene work of the other is a good technique which will undo the stigma of bragging about oneself and will also heighten the feeling that Tom and Leonard work well together and complement each other as a team.

The suggested content and transition flow described thus far in this outline script serve to illustrate how a five-minute documentary can be effectively put together, provided certain directorial considerations are made in advance and the parties concerned are in agreement as to the goal and desired flavor of the finished product.

It is of course important that the documentary contribute to the overall campaign concept of Staisey-Foerster as THE BUILDERS and that it enhance the feeling of the entire campaign as an integrated whole. For this reason, we would probably do well to open on a strong theme of dynamic work in progress, carry this theme along by showing how it is largely the result of the foresight and initiative of our candidates, and close out on a good, strong reference to the BUILDER theme. If we can show that this type of growth and progress has been manifested by a genuine concern for the people of Allegheny County and for their very real and human problems, we should have a successful documentary and a successful campaign.

It is too early to chart an outline script in much more detail than has been done so far. What is written will change, in some places more than in others, as filming progresses and we re-evaluate what we have in the can.

We should make lists of situations to be filmed with the candidates, and we should make sure we have good coverage of these situations. We should make additional lists of public works projects which need to be filmed to show off Staisey and Foerster as THE BUILDERS.

In interview situations, as in situations where the candidates are interacting with the people, good material will come our way as a matter of course, if we have an eye out for it and if we maintain a consistent directorial slant. We know where we're going and what we're after. It is up to us to make the proper things happen on film and to get good filler material for transitions.

So far as narration is concerned, it is too early to write finished stuff.  Narration will be polished and considered carefully when we are in the rough-cut stage and we can see where it is necessary to move things along, and to make points which cannot otherwise be covered. Narration will not be used excessively.  It will be most effective if we can use the candidates and the people themselves to tell the story of Staisey and Foerster, THE BUILDERS.

# PART TWO

# AN AUTOCRAT IN THE WHITE HOUSE

"Donald Trump is a fraud, a fake."
                                    -- Mitt Romney


"This has now become a Trump cult."
                                    -- Senator Bob Corker


"For the first time in my life, we have a president who every day seeks to divide us, not unite us.  It's very disturbing, very depressing."

                                    -- Mike Barnicle, MSNBC

# CHAPTER FOUR

*Capitalism, Socialism and Trumpism*

The term "socialism" has become so successfully demonized by Republicans that their right-wing ideologues foam at the mouth at the mere mention of it.

But the truth is that we don't have either capitalism or socialism in this country; what we have is capitalism with its worst excesses mitigated by socialistic measures, a hard-won blend that has thus far prevented Karl Marx's direst predictions about us from coming true.

Capitalism, socialism and communism are not governmental systems; they are *economic systems* that have to do with who controls the means of production and distribution of goods and services. Democracy and dictatorship are systems for governing, and our democracy is intended to be a system of government "of, by and for the people."

Under the democracy of the ancient Greeks, every citizen voted on virtually any important issue. But that is too unwieldy in a country as large as ours, so we have a republic, theoretically a democracy governed by all of us through our elected representatives.

The three forms of governance that our Founding Fathers feared most were monarchy, theocracy and rule by corporations -- and the latter, personified by the East India Company of colonial times, can be thought of as a precursor of Benito Mussolini's fascism. Under Mussolini, the Italian parliament was called "The Council of Corporations," and the major corporations, instead of the electorate, sent representatives to the Council.

Mussolini's idea was that if the power of the government could be combined with the wealth and power of the corporations, it would be the best of all possible worlds.

We are living under the threat -- and even under the quickly emerging reality -- of de facto fascism in America, due to the fact that we have allowed the multinational corporations, through their highly paid lobbyists and their unbridled use of unprecedented wealth and power, to pay for and own our senators and representatives. Thus they too often write laws that benefit the corporations instead of we the people.

For decades, the corporations and their minions have been relentlessly demonizing that word "socialism" in order to dissuade us from regulating any of their control over us and our democratic institutions.

But what is socialism? It is the idea that there are certain desirable things that can best be accomplished by all of us, working together, through our own representative government. Clean air, clean water, safe foods and medicines, safe and efficient automobiles, safe workplaces, and a well-maintained infrastructure that facilitates travel for pleasure and commerce are just a few of those things. The right to good, effective health care is another.

We the people ought to be able to control the lust and greed of unscrupulous bankers and stockbrokers, and to implement many other wise and efficacious measures that would enhance our "pursuit of happiness" and the general well-being of our nation.  But these kinds of efforts have been consistently blocked by the hired minions of the huge corporations.

A large, ferocious bloc of right-wing ideologues has swallowed the twisted, self-serving corporate propaganda hook, line and sinker.  Wave that dreaded word SOCIALISM in front of them and they not only vote against their own best interests, they are apparently ready to die for their right to be manipulated into supporting the best interests of the one-percent plutocracy that pulls their strings.

Donald Trump is their puppeteer.  The trend toward de facto fascism in this country was growing stronger and stronger before he came into the White House, and now it's on a tear, a rampage, a temper tantrum directed not only toward our own government but also toward our friends and allies all over the world.

It is clear to any insightful person that his slogans, AMERICA FIRST and MAKE AMERICA GREAT AGAIN, are thinly disguised euphemisms that his more extreme idolaters, especially his racists and white supremacists, can  decipher with a knowing wink and a snide smirk. That's why they were so overjoyed when he first got elected, proud of having what they thought was "a man of their own" at last in the White House.

Trumpism is a further mutation of fascism, a narrower and more focused version of it, as Hitlerism was to Nazism: an ideology concentrated in the person of one man, one powerful and charismatic leader.  Heil, Hitler! Heil, Trump!  Donald Trump thinks he is the *boss* of the entire country, not just a president with congressional curbs and limits to his power.  And the present Congress is letting him get away with it.

Hillary Clinton called his followers "a basket of deplorables."  I don't think she should have said that.  It probably made them even madder and cost her many votes, even among people who might otherwise have reluctantly voted for her.  But I think that the worst elements of Trump's political base truly *are* deplorable. I'm talking about the racists.  They surged for Trump because they know, in their heart of hearts, that his campaign slogan really means MAKE AMERICA *WHITE* AGAIN.

The non-racists who fervently support Trump want to go back to a time that in many ways never really existed, except on television: the world of *Andy Hardy, Father Knows Best* and *Happy Daze.*

They are in a happy daze that Donald Trump cynically fostered. They believe his vainglorious claims about himself.  They love his hubris, his lies and his empty promises.  They are desperate to believe in him.  They are hungry for hope.  Even false hope.  False hope that the coal mines and steel mills will boom again.

They don't want to accept the reality that the world of their dreams, the half-fictional past when they had good-paying jobs and lived in mostly white communities, is never coming back again.

Just as Hitler made an unholy alliance with the Pope

and the Catholic church, Trump has made an alliance with the evangelicals, who stifled whatever moral outrage they might have felt about him -- particularly about his abuse of women -- because they hoped they would love his Supreme Court appointments.

The evangelicals also have a strange symbiotic relationship with the Jews, in spite of the fact that they believe no Jew can ever get into their heaven. They applauded Trump's move of the American Embassy from Tel Aviv to Jerusalem, even though it is anathema to the Palestinians and will make the two-state solution more difficult if not impossible.

The evangelicals believe literally in the Old Testament. They think that the End of Days will happen and Jesus will return to rule the earth only when all the Jews return to the Holy Land with Jerusalem as their capital. They also believe that the earth was created 6,000 years ago, never mind all scientific evidence to the contrary.

They don't believe in evolution either, because it contradicts the biblical story of Adam and Eve. I think it's likely that a whole lot of creationists and anti-evolutionists just don't want to accept that we all came from Africa -- it would contradict what they want to think in their heart of hearts: that whites are superior to blacks and blacks are a form of pre-human or subhuman.

People who don't believe in evolution also tend to be climate-change deniers. I wonder if subconsciously this is another way for them to hasten the End of Days? I've seen some of their brainwashed, usually home-schooled, children on television praying for the end of the world, the return of Jesus Christ, and the day when God will "rapture" them into Paradise, leaving unbelievers like me to perish by the millions in eternal fire and damnation.

I don't think Donald Trump truly believes in any religion; he only believes in himself. He's using the evangelicals just as they are using him. It's a rather appalling symbiotic relationship of strange bedfellows.

In any case, I refuse to vote for anyone who doesn't believe in science, doesn't believe in evolution or climate change, and wants the earth to be destroyed so Jesus Christ will come back. That is not a person who should be trusted to have his finger on a nuclear button.

# CHAPTER FIVE

*The Bully in the Pulpit*

I'm not going to pussyfoot around here; I will say it straight out: Donald J. Trump is an enemy of our democracy, unfettered by truth, decency or scruples.  I don't think  he fully understands himself or what he is doing, he is just being what he has been all his life: an habitual liar, a callous manipulator and a ruthless money-grubber.  He is blinded by his lust for power, the power he already managed to get by hook or crook, and his desire to run America like a corporation, or more accurately like a vast political *conglomeration* owned only by *him* and run for the benefit of himself and his family.

Prior to getting into the White House, I don't think that he was ever as rich as he claimed.  I believe his constant claim of being a billionaire was all bluster, all showmanship, like everything else he does.  That is why Lawrence O'Donnell was proven correct when he made the bold prediction back when Trump was first  threatening to run for president, that he would never actually run -- because he was cash poor and badly needed his salary and royalties from *The Apprentice*.

But now America is his slush fund, he's raping the country the way he raped his bankrupt companies, and at last he can truly become the billionaire he always claimed that he was (even when it wasn't literally true yet) and always dreamed that he would be.  High on his love and admiration for himself, and with an ego that constantly needs feeding because of his deep inner self-doubts (because he knows he is a fake), he runs amok like a bull in a china shop, shattering democratic norms, erasing divisions of power, disregarding checks and balances, and using congressional acquiescence to get his own way.

The emoluments clause of the United States Constitution means nothing to him.  He made a career out of raping all of his various enterprises (Trump University being one of the worst and most notorious of his scams). His modus operandi was to stiff his suppliers, contractors and employees, then file for bankruptcy to keep from paying his bills, while constantly lining his own pockets with every brazen maneuver.

He doesn't care about decency, honesty or telling the truth.  As of this writing, according to the *Washington Post* he has told around three-thousand lies from his "bully pulpit" -- a term coined by Theodore Roosevelt back when "bully" used as an adjective meant "excellent."  But now we have a bully *in* the pulpit.  Like a schoolyard bully, he thinks he can get ahead by putting other people down.  He insults and belittles people every day, at his self-adulatory rallies and on Twitter.

He makes fun of a man with his body control made disjointed by multiple sclerosis, a Muslim war hero who gave his life protecting other soldiers, a congresswoman, Tammy Duckworth, who lost her limbs in combat, and of course John McCain, of whom he said, "*He* was captured. I like people who *weren't* captured."  This from a man who claimed five deferments because he supposedly had bone spurs.  One night, Stephen Colbert mocked him for brashly and grandiosely announcing that he was forming a Space Army as a new branch of our Armed Services -- something he has no authority to do, even if it made sense.  Colbert said wryly that Trump probably wouldn't be able to serve in it because of "space spurs."

I used to get a kick out of the times that Colbert would have "Cartoon Trump" as a guest on *The Late Show.* In many ways, he's a cartoon, but a really dangerous one, with whom the danger never goes away.  We laugh but we tremble, as with Charlie Chaplin's long-ago lampoon of Adolf Hitler, who brutally wiped the smiles off of everyone's faces and launched a war and other atrocities that killed a hundred million people.

When I'm not worried that he might kill us all, I can find some aspects of Donald J. Trump absurdly laughable. Sometimes he reminds me of "the Duke" and "the Earl" in *The Adventures of Huckleberry Finn.*  For instance, one day when these two frauds were on their way into a town where they intended to work one of their rip-offs, one of them expressed fear that they would be unmasked, and the other one pooh-poohed him by saying, "Ain't we got *all the fools in town* on our side?  And ain't that a big enough majority in *any* town?"

Trump barked and bullied his way into national political prominence by trumpeting the "birther" lie.  He boasted that he would send a team of investigators to Hawaii to "dig up Obama's real birth certificate."  He said he would prove that Obama wasn't born in the United States and therefore was not a legitimate president but sort of a "Manchurian Candidate."  This contributed to the sad fact that Barack Obama got many times more death threats than any previous president.  Racists who couldn't stand having a black president wore T-shirts portraying him as a gorilla dressed up in a tux.  Some of them sported bumper stickers that said:  VOTE FOR ANYBODY WHITE IN 2016!

During his presidential campaign, Trump said that he could gun somebody down right on Fifth Avenue and his  supporters would still love him. Unfortunately, he was probably right.  We went from having a decent, gracious, articulate man in the White House to electing a man whose coarseness is so brazen and pervasive that we have gotten used to it.  His name-calling alone should have turned all of our stomachs as much as his grabbing of women's private parts.  Some samples of his ignorant put-downs:
"Crooked Hillary."
"Poor Little Marco."
"Lying Ted."
"No-energy Bush."
He's an egoist, a narcissist, who works hard to destroy everyone who disagrees with him or refuses to swear allegiance only to him.  He doesn't understand that this is a nation of laws, not a nation of loyalty to one supreme leader, as in Nazi Germany or North Korea.  He said that everyone should stand and salute when he walks into a room, like the Koreans do for Kim Jong Un.  That's what he wants: love, admiration and adulation, just like all of the world's strong-man dictators.

He thinks only of himself.  He is unable to feel empathy, which is a hallmark of narcissism.  Narcissists and sociopaths cannot feel empathy; however, they can successfully mimic it, glossing it over with charisma or personal charm.  But they cannot truly feel it.

Trump has been tentatively diagnosed as a sociopath by more than two dozen eminent psychologists and psychiatrists. "Tentatively" because they had to do the diagnosis from a distance. But anyone who isn't blinding himself can clearly see that we have a seriously flawed person in the White House.  We don't need to give him a Rorschach Test or a Minnesota Multi-Phasic Personality Inventory.  All we have to do is watch and listen.

Those of us who have not drunk his Kool-Aid can see the symptoms every day in his tweets, his bluster and his incessant use of self-aggrandizing hyperbole.  He is constantly pounding into us  the Big Lie that  everything he does is bigger and better than anything anyone else has done and that the people he surrounds himself with, like his sycophantic political appointees, are the greatest and most amazingly wonderful people in history, even though most of them have been fired and replaced many times over -- by *him*.

The ones who swallow their pride and stifle their consciences to remain loyal to Trump usually manage to keep their jobs by aiding and abetting his wretched excesses and his cruelties, and one of the most abhorrent has been tearing little kids from the arms of their parents and herding them into pens made of chain-link fencing. As I write this we are seeing heart-wrenching scenes of these suffering, crying children night after night on television.

I am not trying to equate Trump's offenses with the crimes against humanity committed by the Nazis in Germany.  I'm not trying to draw a false equivalency.  Yet there are certain tendencies of Trump and his minions that make me wonder just how far they might go if left unchecked.

SS Commander Heinrich Himmler, in charge of Hitler's concentration camps and gas chambers, said, "The wonderful story, the amazing story, the story that can never be told, is how we could have done all this and still have remained decent men."  What an astounding example of the ability of the human mind to compartmentalize guilt and utterly circumvent our "better angels"! Penning up little kids is "kinder" than gassing them.  But it probably requires a similar degree of compartmentalization.  Surely this cannot be happening in America.  Yet it is.

On June 19, 2018, White House correspondent Hunter Walker wrote, "President Trump's controversial child separation policy is being carried out with the help of private businesses who have received millions of dollars in government contracts to help run the shelters where young migrants are being held away from their parents."

Republicans for decades have wanted to privatize every governmental program or agency that they can make a big buck out of -- never mind what happens to America. Private prisons profit by filling cells with inmates warehoused with stiff prison sentences under the three-strikes you're out policy.  Private companies profit big-time by warehousing immigrant children.  And, by the way, Private armies such as Black Water profit immensely from endless war.

The privatization of the Post Office is also on the Republican agenda.  Trump blasts the American postal service in his loudmouthed tweets.  He claims it is losing money.  But it has already been purposely driven into huge financial difficulty, not by its own fault, but by unnecessary burdens contrived by Congress, in what I think is an insidious effort to drive it toward a take-over. Why should an excellently run and highly efficient governmental service be allowed to continue, when tons of money can be diverted into privately owned coffers?

Huckleberry Finn described how The Duke and The Earl were tarred and feathered by an angry mob and ridden out of town on a rail.  We can do that to Trump with our ballots, instead of getting our hands sticky and smelly with hot, messy tar. We don't even have to do it with roars of mockery, the way *he* would probably do it to some of *his* enemies if he had a free hand.

He and his White Nationalists, Stephen Miller and Steve Bannon, and now the ubiquitously, hawkishly warmongering John Bolton, have alienated the rest of the world, our allies and former friends, in a way that Putin could not have done on his own.  Trump has crippled our role in the United Nations as well as in NATO.  Putin must be grinning.

Maybe we won't have to vote Trump out, maybe we can impeach him.  Either way, once he is out of the picture, perhaps we can begin to regain hope for the "kinder and gentler America" that George H.W. Bush once envisioned.

# CHAPTER SIX

*Trump's Army*

Trump has appointed a host of Cabinet Secretaries who have always wanted to destroy the agencies they are purportedly now serving. He has given them the power to do so, and they are going about it with great fervor and efficiency. Scott Pruitt has rescinded the EPA's measures for protecting the environment and guaranteeing us clean air and water. Even while he was still running things in Oklahoma, he was a flunky for the oil companies and one of the most corrupt officials in history, a role he has continued to fill. Maybe by the time this book is published, he will be gone. Just like his leader Donald Trump, he is milking our government for everything he can grab, with the fervor of unconscionable greed.

Betsy DeVos, who happens to be the enormously wealthy sister of the guy who founded Black Water, got exorbitantly rich running a string of private schools and working hard to put public schools out of business. Yet Trump made her his Secretary of Education. Talk about putting the fox in the hen house!

The State Department has already been gutted and debilitated by Trump and his erstwhile Secretary of State

Rex Tillerson who, while he was CEO of Exxon, contrived to derail State Department efforts to keep state-of-the-art armaments out of the hands of ruthless, ambitious and newly oil-rich African dictators.

Trump's army of fervent true believers don't care about any of that.  They don't care if their emperor has no clothes, no empathy and no dignity.

I believe that they are his top priority.  Not getting reelected.  Not creating a lasting legacy as a wise and effective leader.

He wants to create new wealth that continues to grow by means of the self-centered enterprises that have grown and grown and grown in cachet and notoriety because of his ascendancy to the presidency and his gross indifference to the Emoluments Clause.

His "base" (and that's a good adjective for it as well as a noun) will keep on adulating him and making him and his family and their descendants wealthy forever, even if he fails to gain a second term.  That's why he's all about pandering to his base -- the blind and/or greedy forty percent who love and adore him no matter how destructive he is.  They have given him the kind of power that makes "normal" Republicans tremble, even the ones who used to say NEVER TRUMP back when he was a "mere" candidate.

I'm reminded of a scene from my most admired television epic, *Rome*, thirty-five wonderfully written, produced and directed hours, all of which I've watched at least five times, and then I bought both seasons on DVD.

There is an absorbing and enlightening incident in which the feared and politically entrenched older man, Marc Antony, is mustering all of his supposed wisdom to persuade young, inexperienced Octavian that the boy does not have the political connections or expertise to deal effectively with the wise and shifty Roman senators in order to pursue a course of action that Marc believes is unwise.

Octavian listens to all of Marc's logic and reasoning, but is not dissuaded even though the logic is sound. Instead, he replies simply: "I have an army."

So does Trump.  It's the power he doesn't want to lose, even if he loses the presidency.

When talking heads on TV comment in wonder about some of Trump's brash and politically unwise moves, trying to figure out why he would do such things even though they will hurt his chances of getting reelected, I believe that they are missing the point, the real method to his madness.

He'd probably like to get reelected, sure. He'll take it if it comes his way, and he'll even fight for it.

But priority number one is maintaining his army.

# PART THREE

# AMERICA, AMERICA!

Elia Kazan made a movie called *America, America*, about the hopes and struggles of an impoverished immigrant pursuing the American Dream. The title was meant as a phrase of hope and lament. Hope that we may yet continue on a path toward becoming "a more perfect union," and also a lament over the grave imperfections and injustices that threaten to destroy us.

"We were in a different country after those shots rang out in Dallas."

--Tom Brokaw

"I didn't kill anybody."<br>-- Lee Oswald

"No American of that time will forget when, where, how he or she heard the news...we sensed an era had ended...we mourned our lost youth."

-- Theodore H. White

CHAPTER SEVEN

*The Right Wing Divorce from America*

Now that they have "their man" in the White House, the so-called Alt Right is much more content than they were under Obama or Clinton. Back then, they were flooding the Internet with a sarcastic *Divorce Agreement* that they thought was the absolute ultimate in cleverness, pushing their view that America should be partitioned into two separate countries. It listed their reasons for wanting to segregate themselves from the "desperate lefties" that they despised.

They purported that they would let us keep our "liberal judges, homeless folks, hippies, illegal aliens and the ACLU," but they would keep their firearms, their cops, their NRA, their military, their greedy CEOs, their rednecks and their Judeo-Christian values.

To us they would cede NBC, Hollywood, humanism and the United Nations. *They* would continue to believe that health care is a luxury and not a right. *They* would continue to practice trickle-down economics and let *us* "give trickle-up poverty our best shot."

They would keep the *Battle Hymn of the Republic* and the *National Anthem* and allow "the lefties" to keep Jane Fonda and Oprah Winfrey.

I was so incensed by this rabidly insensitive, smug and sanctimonious diatribe that I wrote the following rebuttal addressed to *All hate-filled, embittered, right-wing ideologues:*

The "divorce" and partitioning of America that you propose is basically a good idea, but we disagree on the details.  We counter-propose the following:

(1)  Since the lunatic fringe harbored and applauded by you already has secessionist movements hard at work in Alaska and Texas, you should all relocate to those places. You will feel right at home there.  The rape and murder statistics in those states are the highest in the nation as it is presently constituted, and the opportunities to use handguns, rifles, AK-47's, bazookas and tanks on each other should delight you. Your NRA is perfectly suited to supervise the carnage.

(2)  Once we are rid of you, we promise not to addle your dogmatic brains with any intellectual curiosity.  You can continue to ignore scientific facts and data concerning human evolution and geological history; you will be free to stunt the mental capacity and reasoning power of your children by preaching shallow, unfounded "beliefs" like "creationism" and "intelligent design."

(3)  Similarly, you will be free to warp and distort the intentions and beliefs of the Founding Fathers.  You may

continue to ignore the fact that they gave us a republic based on "freedom of and from religion."  We realize that religious tolerance is anathema to you, and that many of you are already pushing for the establishment of a Taliban-like "Christian" theocracy in America.  We suggest that you elect people like Pat Robertson, Ann Coulter, Rush Limbaugh, Glen Beck and Sean Hannity to head what to us would be a "hell on earth" but to you would be a comforting form of government.

(4)  We will stipulate that you can keep all the greedy corporations, rednecks and intellectually vapid hockey moms that you desire, like Sarah Palin.  We don't want them.  If you change your mind about taking them, perhaps they will be "Raptured" away from us in the near future.  We firmly believe that after all the fanatical religionists, nutty self-serving evangelists and bible thumpers are gone from the earth, it will be a much more pleasant, rational and peaceful home for us.

(5)  You may keep enough weapons to defend yourselves and your homes in Alaska and Texas from us, even though we have no intention of invading.  You may not, however, invade us, killing off thousands of us, as you did in Iraq, under false pretenses.  We find it appalling that after 9-11, when three thousand and more of our innocent citizens were killed by religious fanatics, you compounded the carnage by placing our soldiers into a phony, misguided war where many thousands of them have been needlessly killed, as well as thousands of innocent Iraquis.

(6)  You will refrain from any involvement in international affairs, for when you intrude you are like the proverbial "bull in a china shop," stomping on and wrecking the hard-won vestiges of civilization and human decency that have been achieved by the wise use of compassion, restraint and diplomacy.

(7)  You may keep your so-called "Judeo-Christian values" because your interpretation of those values has always been largely a bastardization of the humility and kindness that Jesus preached.  You may keep your Bibles too, but you really ought to read and understand exactly what is in them and not merely cram your grotesque vision down other people's throats.

(8)  We will stipulate that you can keep all your gas-guzzling, environment-polluting vehicles.  But don't bring them into our new country.  We will try to use our science and our propensity for basing our lives on facts in order to mitigate the pollution from your way of life that will inevitably impinge upon the atmosphere, the water and the earth that we all must share.

(9)  Since we believe that health care is a right and an expression of human decency, and you do not believe this, we will try to accept and care for your sufferers in our hospitals and hospices.  You really ought to agree to pay us for doing this, but we realize that you may not be able to, after your trickle-down economy utterly collapses.

(10)  We don't know why you don't want Hollywood, since it provides much of the pornography that is secretly highly

coveted by your "family value" preachers and politicians, even as they deny their extramarital affairs or homosexual inclinations and pretend that they are morally superior to the rest of us by bashing gays. We will gladly keep Hollywood and all other bastions of creativity. We like and admire our writers, artists, philosophers and poets, and we realize, as you do not, that their deep thinking forms the underpinning of our democracy.

(11) We will keep the army and the Postal Service. We know how much you hate socialistic government-run entities and decry their so-called "inefficiency." You will have to raise your own army or else maybe revive and expand Black Water. Your territory will be smaller now, in square miles, so maybe you will revive the Pony Express or enter into contracts with privately-owned expediters such as Fedex.

NOTE: Although your territory is smaller than ours, it will become less and less crowded as you continue to kill each other off with millions of unregulated pistols, rifles and AR-15's.

(12) You can keep your flags and anthems. Much as we are deeply attached to them, as emblems of our democracy and our way of life, we understand that they are, after all, mere emblems of what we believe in and are willing to die for, and are not the beliefs themselves. Since you value the emblems so much more than you value or understand the principles behind them, we will reluctantly cede the emblems to you, in the interest of facilitating this Agreement.

This Agreement is such an excellent idea, from both of our standpoints, that we really ought to sign it immediately, for we will need some considerable time to allow for the evacuation of Texas and Alaska by those who will be too frightened to stay there after you take over.

Sincerely,
John A. Russo
Freedom Spokesperson

# CHAPTER EIGHT

## *My Dealey Plaza Lament*

I think of Dealey Plaza as a bellwether, a turning point, not just for me and my friends, but for America. It was as if we came all unsuspecting to a fork in the road and got shoved by cataclysm onto a darker, more dangerous path. Things that might have happened did not happen, and other, usually worse, things happened instead.

If President Kennedy had lived to serve a second term, he probably would have pulled our troops out of Vietnam. Lyndon Johnson would not have become president, the war would not have been escalated, and we would not have had the Tet Offensive, the Mi Lai Massacre, and all the other wartime blunders and atrocities that put the names of 58,000 Americans on a black granite wall.

If President Johnson would not have had to step down, Robert Kennedy might not have run for president and might not have been assassinated. Richard Nixon might never have gotten elected, and we might never have heard of Woodward and Bernstein and the Watergate whistle blower named after a porno movie.

That movie, *Deep Throat*, helped to launch a Sex

Revolution that liberated women to do what men wanted them to do and to do it without fear of unwanted pregnancy.

Homicide became the leading cause of death of pregnant women.

Domestic violence reached epic proportions.

Weak, twisted men, scared of assertive women, turned their lusts onto children, and when they were released from prison as registered sex offenders they hunted for more children to rape and kill.

Assassinations and assassination attempts became commonplace. Martin Luther King, Ronald Reagan, John Lennon, George Wallace and Larry Flynt were gunned down.

Angry, bitter people shot complete strangers or co-workers. A new phrase was coined for it: Going Postal.

Serial rapists and mass murderers stalked our streets with near impunity. Prolific killers such as Charles Manson, Ted Bundy and John Wayne Gacey basked in their notoriety and hawked souvenirs of their exploits on the Internet.

The Internet became the blessing and curse of a so-called Information Age that destroyed the slower, calmer patterns of past ages faster than we could comprehend or cope. We wallowed in affluence on the one hand and despair on the other, hooked on methamphetamines, heroin, household inhalants, airplane glue, intolerant religion and extremist politics.

Aimless youth rejected everything our civilization had to offer, except computers, video games and tattoo parlors. They pierced their noses, lips, tongues, navels and labia, as if forming a neo-primitive tribe of their own in lieu of joining the confused, conflicted culture they were born into.

The teenage suicide rate skyrocketed.

Since it was still possible to get richer here than practically anywhere else, and to do it faster and more rapaciously, we believed our boast that we were the Greatest Country on Earth. We kept on trying to make ourselves safe by bombing and killing people in less powerful, less affluent countries.

When suicide bombers attacked us with our own fuel-laden airliners, we ran scared and waxed patriotic and sent our brave young soldiers to die in the wrong place.

Home-grown terrorists sprang up everywhere in our own midst. Timothy McVeigh. The Unabomber. The Columbine Killers. They horrified us with their huge and sudden body counts, shockingly outshining our usual complacent habit of bumping each other off at a slow but sure rate of twenty-thousand per year, with handguns.

Mere handguns weren't enough for us though. Folks scared and enraged clamored for assault rifles, machine guns, even tanks and bazookas. They claimed it was their Constitutional Right. Every crackpot cause had its militia, its militant fringe, and they adamantly felt they must be well armed. Some hated gays, some hated the government, some hated abortionists, some hated evolutionists, some hated anybody whose skin wasn't white.

They said they'd give up their guns when their guns were pried from their cold dead hands.

And so the cold dead hands multiplied.

# CHAPTER NINE

*Shades of Gray*

It occurs to me that people who think that a massive snowstorm is evidence that there is no such thing as global warming are the same people who believe that the shooting in Tucson of Gabby Giffords, along with many other innocent people, had nothing at all to do with the climate of hatred that exists in this country -- the climate that they helped create.

They are many of the same people who want to believe that the earth was created 6,000 years ago. The same people who think that "creationism" is a valid scientific theory, even more valid than the theory of evolution. They find it oh so easy to compartmentalize their thinking. They see black and white instead of shades of gray. The gestalt eludes them. They don't get the big picture, and they don't really want to. It might destroy some of their comforting illusions. It might invalidate their posturing and their sloganeering.

These are the people who carry signs about "watering the tree of liberty with the blood of tyrants" while they openly wear their guns to their rallies to show

how ready they are to use them against the rest of us. They claim they can brandish their firearms and their bellicose attitude without actually inciting anybody to fire the first bullet into an unsuspecting crowd at a theater, a concert, or in a school; in other words, without tipping some confused or mentally deranged person over the edge.

They refuse to learn the lessons of history, not just the broad lessons concerning war and empire that could have precluded the wars in Iraq and Afghanistan, but the more parochial lessons, like the ones that should have taught us that law and order did not come to the Wild West till people were made to stop wearing their guns to town.

Instead, they have brought the Wild West to *all* of our modern towns and cities.

How many guns do they think it will take to make us "safe" from each other? They want to arm everybody, even teachers.

Those who cannot learn from analogy are doomed to learn from catastrophe. They keep causing the same kinds of tragedies and making the rest of us pay.

I think these same people form a large slice of Trump's vaunted "forty percent," his blindly obedient army. I also think he is perfectly suited to be their Judas goat because his mind is just as shallow as theirs. He is not famous for deep thinking. He won't even read his daily intelligence reports. Apparently he doesn't read *anything*. His gut instincts do his "thinking" -- but I don't think any synapses were ever discovered in anybody's abdomen. Yet his "gut" makes his decisions, and that's why they're so ill-founded. His half-baked tweets keep putting us all in a mad helpless scramble, a tail spin in which truth almost doesn't matter anymore.

Sometimes I think that people like him have a congenital defect that makes their mentality immune to nuance.  It might explain why, instead of thinking with any measure of refinement, Trump lumps people and things into crude, cruel categories.  Mexicans are rapists, blacks are gangbangers, immigrants are a scourge on our society.  Apparently he can't trouble himself to judge people according to the "content of their character," instead of where they came from or the color of their skin.

Not long ago there was a sociological study that showed that extreme prejudice can lower the IQ by ten or more points.  It's because prejudice is stubborn, narrow-minded thinking.  It is indiscriminate categorizing of all who look a little different from you, or who think differently.  It narrows your bands of thought.  It substitutes dogma for insight.

It obliterates all the shades of gray.

CHAPTER TEN

*Let me Explain it to Ya, Billo*

While Bill O'Reilly was still on the air, he used to say that he believed in God because he saw the Hand of God in the orderly movements of the earth, the sun, the moon and the tides.  This is an example of the nuance-free sort of "thinking" that I talked about in the previous chapter.  O'Reilly said, "The sun goes up and goes down, and the moon comes out then goes away, and the tides go in and out, and nobody can explain why."

This of course does not prove that there's a God (whether there is one or not).  But it does prove that Bill O'Reilly's understanding of science is as simplistic as his understanding of politics and American culture.

Ignorance or willful denial of science keeps us in the Dark Ages.  It makes people insist that he earth is only 6,000 years old.  It made the Aztecs cut people's hearts out so the sun would come back and make their crops grow.

Some people say there has to be an intelligent creator because somebody had to create the universe.  But maybe there can't *be* nothing.  Maybe there's too much cosmic pressure to make something *happen*.  I'm sort of joshing about that, but not totally.  After all, Einstein proved that energy and mass are interchangeable. Therefore, once you have energy you can explain everything.  But I don't think that energy is an entity that cries out to be worshipped or throws a fit if you eat meat on Friday.

At present, the notion that energy might exist on its own without being willfully created seems preposterously wild and enigmatic.  Maybe someday we will find out that it's not so farfetched.  But maybe not.  There's no guarantee that human beings can know everything.

What we do know is that we live in a universe that is still expanding from the Big Bang.  Perhaps it has expanded and then contracted and then exploded again and again countless times, constantly destroying old formations of the universe and starting new ones.  Fiery shrapnel hurtles through space for billions of years, forming itself into stars and asteroids and planets as the result of being acted upon by centripetal force, centrifugal force, the force of gravity and so on.  The hurtling fragments keep crashing into one another till some of them begin to find relatively stable orbits.  Others keep on winging through space and time, still crashing and exploding, putting craters on the moon and wiping out the dinosaurs.

Do ya get it, Billlo?  The universe is finding order through the inevitable workings of its own unleashed forces.  Things that don't work themselves into some kind of harmony, some kind of order, cease to exist in their momentary form.  The planets and stars that find order maintain that order  -- until they are interrupted by some big thing that comes crashing into them.  That's why we're still threatened by huge asteroids coming too close to the earth.

The Big Bang is a stage in the re-shaping of the universe, a Big Banging and a re-shaping that may have happened many times during the endless eons of time, totally thoughtless about what stage of the process it happens to be in.  The apparent order that we see in the movements of the moon and stars is inevitable.  It's part of the endless machinations of the universe.

Our moon and sun and earth have worked themselves into a temporary harmony that will maintain itself indefinitely if it is not disrupted.  The sun will come up and the sun will go down and the tides will go in and out with regularity in spite of prayers or voodoo chants or the bloody stone knives of the Aztec priesthood.

# CHAPTER ELEVEN

*My Run-ins with Racism*


Growing up in Clairton, Pennsylvania, population 25,000 back then, and home of the world's largest coke works, operated by United States Steel, I was from my earliest childhood made aware that there was a contrived difference between blacks and whites. Contrived by white people. Even as a child, I didn't understand that sort of prejudice; something told me it was wrong.

In those days, Clairton was about twenty or thirty percent black (although now it's more like fifty percent, and the total population of blacks and whites combined is down to around 6,000 due to the collapse of the mills).

My elders in my extended family of mom and dad and grandparents, aunts and uncles made me aware through their stories that people like us, of Italian descent, were hated almost as much as blacks. This seemed stupid and ignorant to me because even in grade school I knew that much of the English language and our laws and institutions and architecture and so on were derived from the early Greeks and Romans.

Yet my dad told me that the Ku Klux Klan tried to drive out him and his parents and siblings when he was a little boy.  Back then they were living "out in the sticks" in a little town called Large, Pennsylvania, which was not large and was only two miles from Clairton and only about twelve miles from downtown Pittsburgh, which was thought of as a far distance from the big city because not many people had cars.

The Klansmen came in trucks and on horseback and shot off guns and burned a cross in my grandparents' yard, but for some reason my grandparents didn't allow themselves to be driven off.  But they despised their neighbors from then on.  My dad must have been traumatized at a young age, and he reacted by developing an oversized pride with an inferiority complex underneath and a tendency to react hatefully toward others.  In other words, racism aimed at *him* turned him into somewhat of a racist.

When I was in seventh grade, a black kid named Norman wanted badly to be my friend. Sometimes he would fall in with me and my pals and follow me home from school.  I had nothing against him, though I didn't know him very well, but I knew my mother would not want to let him into the house because of fear of incurring my father's anger.  He'd still be at the mill when I got home from school, but would always get there as soon as his shift ended at around four o'clock, and his mean streak would come out if he saw a black kid in the kitchen.

Norman came right inside without asking one of the days when he followed me home.  My mom was nice to him but on pins and needles hoping he'd be gone by the time my father came home.

None of this kind of prejudice made sense to me -- it made me really uncomfortable and I agonized over it.

I eventually learned that a lot of the antipathy toward blacks by the steelworkers, like my dad and his unionized buddies, was because during strikes black men had been recruited in the South and brought to Clairton in railroad cars to take the white guys' jobs as strikebreakers. So the whites called them "nigger scabs." But they were just trying to support their families as best they could, not unlike the desperate immigrants of today, who are now denigrated and dehumanized by Donald Trump.

In the early sixties after I graduated from college and was trying to find a teaching job, I was interviewed by the superintendant of a school system in Mt. Pleasant, Pennsylvania, only about thirty miles from Pittsburgh. The interview was *not* pleasant. The guy said he'd like to hire me but he couldn't do it because his school board hated Italians, fearing they were "Black Hand." My dad, who had been waiting for me in his car, wanted to stomp into the school and "knock that guy on his ass." I had to talk him out of it. Ironically, though he hated prejudice against his own heritage, he himself was still a racist when it came to blacks.

While I was in the army there was an incident of Southern redneck prejudice that I recounted in my autobiography, *My Life with the Living Dead.* It happened when I was in basic training in Fort Jackson, South Carolina. I was in with a bunch of rednecks from Georgia who were National Guard troops. They called me "the perfessor" and ragged on me for reading books. They looked down on the black guys in the battalion and hated the Puerto Ricans. They didn't understand that Puerto Ricans were Americans. One particularly stupid oaf said to me in a slow, dumb drawl, "If they's Amurricans how's come they don't *talk* like Amurricans?"

I had a friend named Harvey Keen, a nineteen-year-old black kid, three years younger than I was at the time. He was only five-seven and a hundred-and-ten pounds, but he had lots of guts and determination.  He never faltered on any of the tough physical tests that we had to face, whether it was crawling under barbed wire with machine guns firing over our heads or stabbing and clubbing our way through the bayonet course.  When we went on our twenty-mile march we had to do it while shouldering rifles and carrying eighty-pound packs, almost as much as Harvey weighed, but he kept pace as well as much bigger troopers.

When we were out on maneuvers there were volunteer boxing matches during breaks.  I had boxed quite a bit, informally, in grade school and high school.  In fact, with a close friend of mine I had built a makeshift boxing ring in the woods and he taught me a lot of what he was learning in the semi-pros.

At Fort Jackson I vowed not to ever box because if I got hurt and disabled for any length of time, I'd have to go through basic training all over again.

But some of the rednecks goaded little Harvey Keen into taking on a big, mean bully who outweighed him by seventy-five pounds, and Harvey had too much guts to back down.  The bully kept hitting him hard and knocking him to the ground, but he kept getting right back up until finally our commander stopped the match -- but Harvey was badly hurt and trying not to show it.

It pissed me off so much that I volunteered to take

on one of the toughest brawlers in the battalion.  His last name was Bragg and he was a bruiser.  The rednecks gawked at me in disbelief and said things like, "You gotta be stupid, perfessor!  You gonna step in there with *Bragg?*"

But it turned out that although Bragg was strong as a bull he had few boxing skills.  He tried to dominate with brute strength.

I kept dodging and weaving, keeping my jab going, bang, bang, bang, over and over, and luckily for me it was enough to make Bragg appear totally outclassed.  I didn't knock him out but clearly won.  Then the rednecks said things like, "Tell the truth, perfessor, you're Golden Gloves!"

After that, they stopped picking on me, and better yet they stopped picking on Harvey Keen.  But they still gaped at him in wonderment each time he bowed his head and said Grace in the mess hall.  They couldn't get over the fact that he was more diligent in his prayers than they were, when he was black and they were white and superior to him in their own minds.

After Basic, I was stationed at Fort Bragg and there was a young black soldier named Green who had fleshy lumps on his face that looked like lymphomas.  That might have been part of the reason, in addition to the color of his skin, that a group of sergeants took to picking on him.  After weeks of this, they finally piled up a bunch of petty or fictitious so-called "infractions" that were enough to hit him with a Dishonorable Discharge.

He was in the Orderly Room, his duffle bag packed, and in tears waiting for a jeep to take him to the stockade, when I asked the first sergeant what was going on -- then angrily spoke up for Green.  I told how he had been picked on for months for no reason and said I would testify on his behalf if he got court-martialed.  This made the first sergeant and the captain back down.  Luckily they considered me a company asset and knew I was articulate enough to make them look bad in front of a court of battalion officers.  So they let Green off the hook and he completed his enlistment and got out of the army.  I still remember how he cried when he thanked me, and I have always been glad that I had the nerve to defend him.

I despised Fort Bragg.  It was the home of the brave and famous (and I'm being admiring, not sarcastic here) 82nd Airborne Division, and a lot of the airborne troops hated us because we didn't jump out of planes. They called us "legs" and ganged up on some of us anytime they could.  Quite a few guys got the crap beat out of them when they went into Fayetteville.  Also, for some reason, that army town was hostile to soldiers in a big way, even though the post put them on the map and was a big boost to their economy.  Many of the lawns had signs that said *Soldiers and Dogs, Stay off the Grass!* And we got gouged in all the bars, where we could watch gorgeous Korean girls, who were the wives of the noncoms who brought them over here, dancing half naked on a small stage.  But in my experience it was always *Look, don't touch.*  And if you spent all your money drinking and couldn't pay for any more, you were ordered to leave so someone with money could take your stool.

When James Meredith, a black man, attempted to enroll in Ol' Miss, almost all of Bragg's Military Police were sent there to prevent riots, and I was assigned to temporary MP duty.  My job was to work the army desk in the basement of the Fayetteville jail, and my supervisor was a disabled MP sergeant who had been pressed into duty due to the crisis in Oxford, Mississippi. He was authorized to carry a .45 automatic, and I wasn't, even though I was the one who had to go up on the elevator once each hour to check on the guys in the cells, because he was too frail to do it.

Almost every night forty or so troops, mostly airborne, would be locked up for offenses ranging from drunk and disorderly to public lewdness to assault with deadly weapons. And I was required to actually open the cell doors each time I went up there to make sure none of them had killed one another or hanged themselves. The reason I had to unlock the cell doors to peer in was that the solid steel doors didn't have any apertures. And if anything bad happened on my watch, I'd be court-martialed. Most of the time, as soon as I swung one of the cell doors open, I'd find myself face to face with one of the inmates staring at me. Since I carried no weapon other than the stubby length of broomstick that the key dangled from, any one of them could have strangled me and fled, utilizing the elevator that I came up on.

These kinds of incidents are just a few highlights of racist occurrences in my own life. Anyone with any degree of awareness does not try to deny the pervasive racism that still exists.

Trump, on the other hand, derides those who know that the civil rights struggle must still go on. He apparently believes that Black Lives Matter is an empty cause and that its marchers should stay home because they don't have anything to complain about.

I don't think that Donald Trump ever experienced racial prejudice directed against *him* -- just on the dishing-it-out side.  His father, Fred, was arrested at a KKK rally in 1927 but released without being charged, and it remains unclear as to whether or not he was a supporter or member of the KKK or merely an observer.  However, both Fred and his son Donald were sued in the 1970's because although they owned hundreds of apartments in New York City only seven of them were occupied by black families.  Some of Fred Trump's employees at that time said that they were ordered to put a "C" on applications from "colored people" so they could be weeded out.

I also have read that Fred Trump, whose last name was originally Drumpf, probably changed at Ellis Island, used to tell the lie that he was from Switzerland, not Germany, because he was afraid that Jews in Manhattan would not want to rent or buy from a German.

Of course nowadays Donald Trump acts like the media are prejudiced against *him* -- but they are not.  Like me, astute and insightful media people cannot stomach what he is doing to America.  He is destroying our democracy, and we are appalled by that.  And the Republicans in Congress are not willing to stand up to him.  They are afraid of his army of fanatical supporters.

There is a strong element of racism among Trump's supporters. Rob Reiner said, "Twenty-five percent of them are racists, and they don't want more brown people coming to America."  Some of them that I know personally take it for granted that any white person will automatically be glad that Barack Obama isn't president anymore.  I have heard them say that no matter what they disagree with Trump on, "He's better than the nigger."

Yet, Republicans cynically assert that there is no longer racism in America and the fact that we had a black president proves it.

But that black president was hated more than any other by a large segment of the population while he was in office.  On *NBC Miami* in 2009, Andrew Greiner said, "A new Biblical Obama slogan making the rounds on conservative T-shirts and bumper stickers is being interpreted as calling for the president's death."

The article was illustrated by a photo of the slogan on a shirt: a pair of praying hands, then the phrase PRAY FOR OBAMA, PSALM 109.8.

Greiner went on to explain, "The phrase seems innocent enough, but the actual verse reads: "Let his days be few; and let another take his office."  The psalm goes on to say:"May his children be orphans, and his wife a widow."

Nice stuff. Bible thumpers prove once more that scripture can be found to accommodate any sort of malice and madness that one wishes to promulgate.

CHAPTER TWELVE

*A Lesson Against Racism from Huckleberry Finn*


Ernest Hemingway said, "All modern American literature comes from one book by Samuel Clemens called *The Adventures of Huckleberry Finn.*"

Some people would like to see that book banned or expurgated because of its realistic and artistic re-creation of idiomatic language in use by Southern whites and blacks of its time period. But Clemens (Mark Twain) was not a racist; he was a *realist* who wanted his literature to depict *life* with all its love, hatred, beauty and ugliness.

In a passage where Huck is going to sneak into a town and the escaped slave, Jim, is afraid Huck might tell on him or at the least not come back to the raft, Huck agonizes with his conscience and his dawning realization of Jim's humanity. Here are excerpts of that passage in Huck's words, and if Donald Trump ever read anything he might learn from it:

*   *   *


Jim talked out loud all the time while I was talking to myself. He was saying how the first thing he would do when he got to a free state he would go saving up money and never spend a single cent, and when he got enough he would buy his wife...and then they would both work to buy the two children, and if their master wouldn't sell them they'd get an ab'litionist to go and steal them.

It most froze me to hear such talk...here was this nigger, which I had as good as helped to run away, coming right out flat-footed and saying he would steal his children -- children that belonged to a man I didn't even know, a man that hadn't ever done me no harm...

He jumped up and got the canoe ready... and as I shoved off he says:  "Pooty soon I'll be a-shoutin' for joy...Jim won't ever forgit you, Huck, you's de bes' fren' Jim's ever had..."

I was paddling off all in a sweat to tell on him; but when he says this, it seemed to kind of take the tuck all out of me...

(When Huck gets confronted and almost shot by slave catchers, he goes against his conscience and doesn't tell on Jim, then he agonizes over his lie that his friend on the raft was white.)

They went off and I got aboard the raft, feeling bad and low, because I knew very well I had done wrong, and I see it warn't no use for me to try and do right; a body that don't get started *right* when he's little ain't got no show -- when the pinch comes there ain't nothing to back him up and keep him to his work, and so he gets beat.  Then I thought a minute, and says to myself, hold on; s'pose you'd 'a' done right and give Jim up, would you feel better than what you do now?  No, says I, I'd feel bad -- I'd feel just the same way I do now.  Well, then, says I, what's the use you learning to do right when it's troublesome to do right and ain't no trouble to do wrong, and the wages is just the same?  I was stuck.  I couldn't answer that.  So I reckoned I wouldn't bother no more about it, but after this always do whichever come handiest at the time.

*       *       *

On top of anything else it teaches, this passage is an excellent example of how children can be schooled from birth to believe in just about anything that adults want them to.  Even the so-called "superiority" of their own skin color.  Even hating or enslaving or wanting to beat or kill anybody who is different from them in any way.

Huckleberry Finn was an unschooled boy pretty much ignorant of "book larnin'."  His father was the town drunk and didn't much care about him in any meaningful or fatherly way.  The mean old man took pleasure in beating Huckleberry with a strap and keeping him locked up in a rude cabin in the woods, which is why the boy escaped, met up with the runaway slave, Jim, and headed down the Mississippi on a raft.

Old man Finn was a textbook example of all the prejudices harbored by "poor Southern whites" of his time, the 1830's, before the Civil War.  But in some ways, not much has changed.  White people who are bitter about their own station in life often hate seeing anyone else "getting ahead."

That's a big part of the reason they love Donald Trump's rants against immigrants and the hateful "policies" intended to stop them from coming here. They hate seeing our country becoming more brown and less white, to the point where whites are expected to be less than fifty percent of the population within the next fifty years.

Keeping economically deprived brown-skinned people out is also another form of voter suppression. Most of them tend to vote Democratic, and the Republicans are well aware of that.

Trump and those of his ilk in Congress are quite skilled in using "cultural issues" like religion and skin color to divide us and get us to vote against our own best interests.

Most poor Southerners prior to the Civil War did not own slaves; yet they fought and died to preserve slavery. In other words, to preserve their own sense of superiority over blacks. They didn't have much but at least, in their minds, they had that.

In some ways, not much has changed. And that's what the Civil Rights struggle is all about. We are still trying to live up to our principles and truly be the Land of the Free and Home of the Brave.

## CHAPTER THIRTEEN

*Another Slice of Racism in Reality Based Fiction*

Since I already set the precedent of including a slice of fictional reality from *Huckleberry Finn* in this basically nonfiction book, I can't resist including a passage from my own book, *Dealey Plaza*. Again, this passage is also fictional, but depicts nothing that hasn't happened in a similar way and with similar cruelty to blacks for four hundred years, going all the way back to the days of institutional slavery.

Including the passage here is another way of illustrating how fiction that mirrors real life can affect us deeply and encourage deeper understanding and empathy.

*       *       *

Coleman Jamison was 37 years old, and had worked for 23 years at the general store in the tiny hamlet of Jonesville, 18 miles south of Oxford, Mississippi. To call it a hamlet might be an exaggeration. It consisted mainly of the general store and a gas station at a dusty crossroads, with a few unpainted shacks dotting the countryside roundabout. In 1964 the population of Jonesville was 187 according to a tin sign nailed to a telephone pole by Pete Jones, the owner of the general store.

Pete called Coleman his "store nigger" and always guffawed when he said it because he thought it was a witty pun on the term "house nigger."  Coleman's lot in life wasn't much different from that of an outright slave on one of the plantations of old.  He got paid fifty cents an hour, got fed on leftovers from his boss's table, and wore clothing donated to the black church he belonged to.  He slept on an army-surplus cot in a room at the back of the store, in a narrow aisle between rows of steel shelves full of dry goods and canned goods.  The storeroom had one grimy window, but any sunlight that might have penetrated was mostly blocked out by the stuff on the shelves.  And Bossman Pete didn't like it if Coleman wasted electricity by turning on the naked bulb that dangled from the ceiling.

There were three hooks by the storeroom door.  Two of them held a few of Coleman's most used garments, and one held Bossman Pete's pointy white hood and his white gown with the big red cross on it.

Coleman's chores consisted of mopping, sweeping, cleaning, chopping firewood, toting heavy boxes of merchandise and putting them wherever he was told to, and lugging customers' purchases to the counter or to their vehicles for them if they wanted him to do so, no tips required.  Any and all other kinds of manual labor fell to Coleman also.  For him to be given this job and to be paid "good money" for it was considered by Pete Jones and others in the white community to be a work of genuine Christian charity.  This was not only because Coleman was black but because he was considered "mentally retarded."

But in spite of the fact that folks called him "slow," he caught on that he had seen the old, faded red convertible before -- the one that got towed out of a half-plowed field a week ago, on orders of the two FBI men that all the white folks hated.  He had stood back from a little crowd on the side of the road, catching glimpses of men moving around among the trees a far piece away, where the trees were strung with yellow crime scene tape.  He had left before getting to see what the car looked like, but he saw the tow truck drive in.  He had to leave sooner than he wanted to, because his boss, who was with the crowd of white folks, showed off to them by yelling, "Git back to work, nigger, or I'll take the strap to ya!"

Later that afternoon, the tow truck pulled into the store's gravel lot and two big-bellied white men got out to buy cans of cold soda pop and to jaw with Bossman Pete for a spell.  Coming outside to fetch the sodas, Coleman recognized the car they were towing -- but he knew better than to pipe up about it.  The tow truck men had perpetual sneers on their faces to show how mean and dangerous they were.  One of them tripped Coleman after he handed them their sodas, and when he fell and skinned his hands and knees they called him a clumsy nigger and laughed so hard the soda pop sprayed out of their mouths.

Bossman Pete and his cronies, plus many other white people, started treating Coleman worse after everybody found out about the murders and body burnings that had happened nearby.  Instead of being angry and scared over the horror of it all, they seemed to be secretly or even openly pleased, as if the victims had gotten what they deserved. Bossman Pete was one of the worst.

He said, "Damn Yankees come down here tryin' to git our niggers all riled up, and instead they got theyselves *fried* up!"

Coleman thought carefully about who he should tell about the red car.  He finally decided he'd tell Reverend Staisy, pastor of the River Jordan Colored Baptist Church down the road.  But he'd have to wait till Sunday when he went to services, or till the next time the reverend came to the general store, which could take a while.

As it happened, Reverend Staisy and his daughter showed up on the same day the car had been towed, but later on when the sun was low in the sky.  Coleman was nervous and tongue-tied around seventeen-year-old Correlle Staisy because she was so pretty.  He knew he was considered ugly, especially by white people.  His skin was very dark.  His lips were thick but the bottom one was thicker than the upper one and stuck out like a nubby shelf over his receding chin.  He had bulging eyes, and the left one had an odd black spot on the white part of it that nobody knew the reason for.  He was only about five-feet-four and a hundred and nineteen pounds, but he was wiry and much stronger than he looked, and when Bossman Pete made him help build a garage, the bossman said, "That little nigger can carry a hod of bricks up a ladder like nobody's bidness.  Why, I believe he c'd outdo most white boys twice his size -- must be the gorilla in him."

There was a sink and toilet in the general store, but it was for white folks. Bossman Pete made Coleman use a plastic basin to wash himself, and he had to do it in the storeroom, setting the basin on his cot. When he needed to go Number One or Number Two, he must do it in the woods out back where nobody could see him.

On the day that Reverend Staisy and his daughter Correlle came by, Coleman waited till it looked like they were ready to leave with their packages, then he asked permission to "go out back for a minute," which was a euphemism for having to empty his bladder.  "Don't you let this purty l'il gal see you or she might get all worked up!" Bossman Pete snickered, and a couple of white customers who had just come in snickered right along with him, lewdly ogling Correlle all the while, smirkingly confident that she and her father would swallow whatever insults were hurled at them, without daring to give back any sass.

Shyly turning his eyes from Correlle to the reverend, Coleman stammered, "Uh...uh...I c'd he'p tote somethin' f-f-fer y'all since I's about to go out."

"Much obliged," Reverend Staisy murmured.  He handed Coleman two bags of groceries, and Correlle went out ahead of them and held the door open.

As they crossed the gravel lot, Coleman glanced all around, then said under his breath, "Reverend, I done seed the red car those gov'ment men was lookin' at."

"Out in the field?  When it was being towed?"

"No, suh, afore that."

The reverend blinked his eyes, a grim look on his face as he stopped by his battered old Chevy. Unlocking the door without looking directly at Coleman, he pretended he was just going about his normal business, in case anyone was watching.  At the same time, he said in a lowered voice, "Are you sure, Coleman?"

"Yessuh, I seed it by the bridge down the road a piece."  He handed  Reverend Staisy the groceries, one bag at a time, and added, "There was a girl with a baby sittin' inside of it, and the girl looked sceered.  Some policemen was arrestin' two white men who mustaa been with 'er -- and a colored man and woman, too."

"Better not say nothin' about it," Correlle said, biting her lip.

The reverend's eyes darted around sharply, then he asked, "When did you see this, Coleman?"

"I dunno, c'd be ten days ago, mebbe.  Shook me up and stuck in my head, but I dint know zackly what was happenin'.  Men with guns waved us on by.  I's sittin' in the bed of Mista Pete's pickup makin' sure some big cans of tar and tarpaper stayed put.  Nothin' I c'd do about what I seed."

"Listen to me, Coleman," Reverend Staisy said sternly. "Don't tell anyone what you saw till I think this all over.  You hear me?  This information could get somebody killed."

"Like us," Correlle whispered.  "We better just forget about it, push it out of our minds."

Coleman was about to stammer an apology for letting them know stuff they didn't want to know, when Bossman Pete banged open the front door of the general store and yelled, "Git yer black ass in here, nigger!  What y'all jawin" about out here?  What's that sneaky look doin' on yer face?  You swipe somethin' from me?  I pick through them bags of groceries and find somethin' nobody paid fer, y'all gonna have hell to pay!"

"We didn't steal nothin', Mister Pete," the reverend said.

"Well, you better git yer black asses outta here!  You got what you came fer -- now *git!*"

Coleman forgot all about his excuse for going outside, which was to go back in the woods to urinate. Instead, he hustled back across the gravel lot, wondering if he was going to get a few licks from Bossman Pete's leather strap. On his way, not daring to look over his shoulder, he heard Reverend Staisy's worn out engine grind a couple of times before it turned over, and the crunch of gravel as the car rumbled onto the blacktop.

Late that night, Bossman Pete, Cletis Barrett and Albert Crane burst in on Coleman as he was kneeling by his cot in the dark, saying his bedtime prayers. Pointing guns at him and yanking him to his feet, they immediately started beating him. Bossman Pete and Albert Crane held Coleman up while Cletis Barrett delivered punch after punch. When he crumpled to the floor, they tied his wrists and ankles with rope. Then they dragged him half-conscious out back into the woods.

"I'll whale into him with my belt till he fesses up," Bossman Pete said.

"Cigarette burns are better," Albert said. "Big fire later on'll cover up what we done."

The cold of the late April evening and the descending fog made Coleman come to. The white men's breath was white, and they were wearing the kind of warm clothing and boots used by hunters. Meekly he muttered through his pain, "Why you doin' me this way, Mister Pete? Whatchou think I done wrong? I dint steal nothin' no way."

"I know you didn't, you wouldn't have the guts," Bossman Pete barked. "But you blabbed about somethin' to that black-ass preacher and his daughter, and we wanna know what it was."

Albert Crane and Cletis Barrett both lit up cigarettes and got the ends glowing red hot.

"U...I d-dint tell 'em nothin', Coleman said pleadingly. "Talked about the w-w-weather is all."

"Bullshit! How dumb you think I am? You made an excuse to go out and piss -- then you come back in without pissin'."

"I's s-s-sceerred when you yelled at me, figgered I b-b-better jest h-h-hold it in."

"I ain't buyin' it -- you three was huddled together like thieves. Guilt was written all over yer black faces."

Albert Crane took a puff on his cigarette to make it stay real hot. A sinister look on his face, he said, "I don't like that l'il black speck on his eyeball. He'd look better with it burnt off."

"Please, n-no, d-d-don't do me that way, suh," Coleman said, cringing. "I d-d-doesn't know n-n-nothin' 'bout nothin' important...neither does Reverend Staisy. We's just jawin' 'bout the weather, the c-crops and such."

"I told you don't bullshit me," Bossman Pete said.

"You ain't nothin' but a lyin' nigger," snarled Cletis Barrett.

"Hold him down, I'll burn him," said Albert Crane.

The other two men sat on Coleman's chest and legs, and Albert Crane knelt beside him and touched the hot red tip of his cigarette against the side of Coleman's neck.

Coleman had the desperately nutty idea that maybe if he showed a lot of guts and did not scream, the men would have more respect for him and would start believing what he told them.

He tried hard not to scream but did not succeed.

"Mebbe we oughta gag him," Cletis Barrett suggested.

"Then how's he gonna tell us what we wanna know?" Bossman Pete said. "Just keep goin'. Nobody around to hear him anyways."

"Yeah, I still wanna burn that black speck," Albert Crane said. "Like a doctor burnin' off a wart."

"Better talk right now, Coleman," Bossman Pete urged. "Unless you itchin' to become a blind man."

Perspiration flooded out of Coleman, and he started to shake all over. His granddaddy, who had lived to be 93, had been 18 years old when slavery ended in 1863, and up till then he had been a slave working in the cotton fields. From him Coleman had heard lots of stories about the cruel punishments that the plantation owners and their overseers had inflicted upon hapless human beings. Black men were beaten to death and their women raped. Runaways were branded when they were caught, or made to wear iron collars welded around their necks. And slaves who persisted in running away sometimes had their feet chopped off; and if that didn't pacify them, they were hanged, their corpses left to rot in the hot sun for days on end, as a warning to others who might be tempted to flee on their own or somehow hook up with abolitionists from up North who were running something called the Underground Railroad. Those kinds of Yankees were shot or hanged when Southern men caught them, or else they were tortured to death.

Coleman realized deep down that Bossman Pete and his two ugly henchmen were living reincarnations of their exceedingly cruel ancestors. They were upholders of an insanely devilish tradition of hatred and white supremacy. And he knew he could expect no mercy from them.

They meant what they said.

There was no escape.

They were going to burn his eyes out...

# PART FOUR

# ROBBER BARONS REINCARNATED

"Nobody can beat me on the economy (and jobs)."
-- Trump Tweet

"I will bring jobs back to the U.S. and keep our companies from leaving.  Nobody else can do it."
-- Trump Tweet

"I'm the only one who knows how to build cities."
-- Trump Tweet

# CHAPTER FOURTEEN

*Trump's Tax Scam*

So here we go again with *Trickle Down!*  Been there, done that, and it led to economic collapse.  So let's try again and again what doesn't work, like a dumbfounded nation that keeps trying to fit a square peg in a round hole.

Back when the unions finally forced employers to pay decent wages, people had money to buy things and send their kids to college, with usually the father working only one regular job and the mother staying home, where, thanks to the lack of work-saving appliances that we now take for granted, the "woman of the house" had plenty of punishingly difficult tasks to labor at, like washing clothes with an old-fashioned washer with a muscle-operated ringer and hanging them out to dry on a rope strung between poles.

Henry Ford, who in addition to being an automotive genius was also a fan of Adolf Hitler (as was Charles A. "Lucky Lindy" Lindberg). Ford was a stern, iron-willed task-master over the men who worked his assembly lines. It was his wife and his factory manager who argued him into raising their wage to at least five dollars an hour back when most millworkers were only getting a dollar and a half.  It was a profoundly iconoclastic and mutually beneficial move, as Mrs. Ford had predicted.  Now the ordinary workers could afford to buy the Tin Lizzies they helped make, and Henry Ford became many times wealthier than he had ever been before.

That's an example of a Trickle *Up* economy!  And it's a reason why we need to raise the minimum wage.

But instead of doing just that, or doing anything else that might benefit the disappearing middle class and the burgeoning number of poor people in this country, Trump and his allies are raping them and grabbing every penny they can for themselves.

The "Tax Reform" bill they passed is more like a Tax Deformed Bill.

Everybody knows it benefits the top one percent to the detriment of everybody else.  And to the detriment of America.  American education, American infrastructure, American health care and Social Security, American just about everything except the American military.  And the American politicians in office.

They know full well that the money they grab now is worth a lot more than any money they or their offspring might get down the line.

Why?

Because it will be growing from now and probably forever to the vast benefit of them and their progeny.

There is a rule, called the Rule of 72, which is a way of calculating for a certainty how much a chunk of invested money will grow on a percentage basis.  You just divide the rate of interest it is earning into 72.

If, for instance, the money is in an annuity with an 8 percent rate of return, 8 into 72 is 9 so the money will double every nine years.

So if the new tax bill gives a congressman a windfall of $100,000 and he puts it into a mutual fund that averages a rather modest 8% over the long haul, which is not out of line with the usual trends, nine years from now the congressman will have $200,000, then $400,000 at the end of the second nine years, and $800,000 at the end of the third nine-year period, and so on. He's probably a millionaire already, thanks to the office he holds and the tremendous perks that come with it, and he'll be a double millionaire twenty-seven years from now -- even if he gets booted out of office in the meantime -- because he has already prudently grabbed that money while he could, and while the rest of us suffered and a lot of us have worked two or three jobs and our wives or husbands did the same, just to barely get by.

The next chapter is an article I once wrote proposing a way that the Rule of 72 might be used to benefit every American citizen.

## CHAPTER FIFTEEN

*The Real and Forever 15% Tax Break*

When Robert Dole ran for president, he said he had a way to give everybody a 15% tax break, and he was ridiculed for saying something that a lot of people thought was so outlandish that he'd never get elected.  As we know, he didn't.  I didn't vote for him either.  But I did think of a way that his 15% tax break might work for real.

I'm not totally sure it'd work, even though it makes sense to me.  But I'm not an economist or a financial wizard, and I'd like to get their input, so I'm putting the idea forward.  It's based on the aforementioned Rule of 72.

What if we could eliminate the Social Security tax? What if we could get rid of our wobbly, excruciatingly expensive Social Security system and replace it with a system that will work forever and never need bailed out?

Every corporation in this country would save 12.4% in taxes on all its employees.  Every self-employed person would save about 15%.

The new system I have in mind takes advantage of the primary and most effective method of building wealth: compounding interest.  We all know that the money we invest earliest will grow the most by the time we retire, yet the present Social Security system totally ignores that knowledge.  Our contributions are based on our annual income, and since we have our greatest earning power when we're at middle age or beyond, we end up contributing the *most* dollars when those dollars have the *least* time to grow.

It would be far better if we could contribute fewer dollars, but do it *early*. As early as possible.  As early as the day we're born.

What if each child born in America had $1,000 salted away for him as soon as he came into the world? Stick with me while I explain how marvelously that money would grow over the child's lifetime.  And I'm also going to explain where we're going to get that money to make it start growing in the first place.

The Rule of 72 gives us an easy way of calculating how long it will take for any investment to double.  You just divide 72 by the percentage of interest your money is earning, and the result equals the number of years it will take for your money to double.  Therefore, if a newborn baby has $1,000 invested for him at 9% interest, it will double every eight years as follows:

| Investment | Investor's Age |
|---|---|
| $1,000 | 0 |
| $2,000 | 8 |
| $4,000 | 16 |
| $8,000 | 24 |
| $16,000 | 32 |
| $32,000 | 40 |
| $64,000 | 48 |

| $128,000 | 56 |
| $256,000 | 64 |
| $512,000 | 72 |

You can see that with a "measly" $1,000 investment for each baby at birth, everyone in America would be able to retire at age 72 with over a half million dollars to support his or her retirement.  If the money could be invested at 10% instead of 9%, they'd all be able to retire around age 63.

Now the Big Question:  Where would the $1,000 come from?  From the parents.  They would forgo their tax deduction of $600 per child for as many years as it would take to compensate the government for the $1,000 it put up.  The $1,000 investment, if need be, could be increased modestly to keep pace with projected inflation, so that later generations would build a larger retirement fund as may be required by inflation.

This program would have many advantages besides enabling us to phase out a system that is always going broke even though we all pay into it at a rate approaching 15% per year.  Some of these advantages are:

(1)  It would eliminate the Social Security bureaucracy.  The $1,000 could be invested with brokerages and/or insurance companies, in an annuity or whatever other financial vehicle makes the most sense.

(2)  Every American citizen and corporation would get a huge tax cut because the current Social Security tax would no longer be necessary.

(3)  It would automatically make savers and investors out of every American, whereas currently people

in this country save less than people do in most other developed countries.  The invested capital would be working for us all, creating wealth for this nation and making it easier for us to compete with other nations.

(4)  It would bestow real "social security" upon us all, freeing us once and for all from retirement worries.

(5)  It would transform late retirement into more of a goal than a much-resented possibility -- because everyone would know that he could double the value of his nest egg merely by working another seven or eight years.  The older one got, the *more* secure one could become, instead of the reverse.

Finally, and as an important added bonus, this plan could contribute toward the solving of the health-care and long-term care crises.  The pool of money accumulated for each individual could be used toward health care or nursing home care, thus reducing the burden currently assumed by taxpayers when people need this care but have little or no money to pay for it.

# CHAPTER SIXTEEN

*Trump's Trumped-up Rants*

It annoys me when talking heads on TV dub Donald Trump a "master of media manipulation" or a "master of diversion" or a "political genius." It makes the public believe he's much smarter or more intelligent than he really is. He's a master of nothing, not even the so-called *Art of the Deal.* He's just more crass, brazen and self-serving than any president has ever been. And he's got a spineless Congress to kiss his ring. Plus a Supreme Court full of his own appointees who will surely almost always do his bidding.

He has combined oligarchy with plutocracy and with himself as head of state, almost as a monarch or a dictator. Plus he's got heavy backing from the Religious Right, especially those who would love to see the United States of America become a theocracy. This is the worst of all possible worlds. And I don't think he's created it with much forethought or insight; it's just a miscreant spawned by his own twisted ego and unbridled hubris. Thanks to him, we have blurred and come close to vanquishing the Separation of Church and State to a level that would have made our Founding Fathers start a second Revolution.

Here are some dictionary definitions:

*Oligarchy:* Government by a small group; a ruling minority.

*Plutocracy*: Government by a *wealthy* minority.

*Monarchy:* Government by a sovereign; a supreme ruler; a potentate.

*Theocracy:* Government by God or his priests.

The Roman Catholic Church never gave up any power that was not wrested from it, usually at great cost in human lives. The Protestant Reformation started by Martin Luther began the erosion of that power. If the theocrats still had all the power they used to have, they'd still be burning witches. And to this day they are still hammering and clawing to hang onto their wishful supremacy over all other religions and beliefs. In a 2016 article in the *Cleveland Plain Dealer*, Tom Ehrich wrote: "The Vatican's pronouncement last week that Roman Catholicism is the only 'instrument for the salvation of all humanity,' and that all other Christians are 'deficient,' and Anglican and Protestant churches 'are not churches in the proper sense,' is so pathetic it seems cruel even to mention it.

"But, Jesus himself issued no laws, established no hierarchies of power, openly refused to proclaim doctrines or to erect barriers against this group or that. He did none of what later Christians claimed was essential.

"A doctrine of 'papal infallibility' would sound absurd to a gentle man who wanted to be called 'teacher' or 'friend,' not 'master.' Furious scouring of Scripture for verses to throw against gays or women or Africans or Aztecs would horrify a rabbi who told self-serving hypocrites to be silent."

Donald Trump is one of those self-serving hypocrites in a secular as well as a religious sense. I don't think he has any solid morals or principles, except to always do whatever is best for Donald Trump. That is why he was so anxious to become such a "strange bedfellow" to the Religious Right.

He now mouths the name of God at prayer breakfasts and other presidential happenings when he can deduce that a large chunk of his following depends on it.

Meanwhile he cynically latches onto any rant that can gain a knee-jerk reaction from his staunchest admirers and supporters.

## The Flag Hugger

Although I'm an army veteran, it actually somewhat annoys me when people say, "Thank you for your service," which has relatively recently become the right thing to say when you meet a veteran. I think most of the people who say it would never put on a military uniform if they could in any way avoid it. But it's easy enough for them to thank a veteran and put plastic *Support the Troops* ribbons on their car trunks.

In spite of his own lack of unselfish service to anybody, either in the military or in his civilian life, Donald Trump has become the Flag Waver in Chief. He has whipped people up against the NFL and the football players, mostly black, who decided to "take a knee" during the playing of the National Anthem. Of course he knows they're mostly black, and I suspect he also knows that a good many white folks, especially the redneck kind, will say, "These black athletes, they're all rich as hell, why should they be disrespecting the flag of the country that gives them contracts worth millions of dollars?"

In other words, I think there's an element of racism in Donald Trump's blathering.  The truth is that *nobody* is "disrespecting the flag."

On the contrary, these professional football players are calling attention to the bald fact that so far we have failed to live up to our claim that we are "the home of the free and land of the brave."  When Francis Scott Key wrote those lyrics, only white male property owners could be said to be free.  Poor whites weren't.  Women weren't.  And slaves and indentured servants certainly weren't.

We've come a long way since then, but blacks still aren't as free as whites, and they are killed unnecessarily by police far more often than whites are.

The NFL players are not raising clenched fists in the air, like the proponents of Black Power used to do.  They aren't yelling and complaining.  They are *kneeling* in front of the flag, respecting it, not *dis*respecting it, while trying to make all of us understand that there are still things that must be done, on our way toward a more perfect union.

I almost lost one of my best friends because of this issue.  He came into the bar at our American Legion post and said, "Rocky Bleier has an excellent point.  He said that the stadiums are a workplace, and ordinary people aren't allowed to demonstrate in *their* workplaces, so the football players shouldn't be allowed either."

I said, "That's a false analogy."

And he exploded on me and  kept yelling at me and telling me to go home. I told him to go to hell.  And we didn't speak for weeks, till finally we talked it out and we're friends again.  A happy outcome.  But if it proves anything, it proves how right Trump's maliciousness  was to seize on this particularly hot-blooded issue to further divide and alienate the American people from each other and make his base love him all the more.

When I said to my friend that Rocky Bleier's rap was a false analogy, I meant that most people don't work in a place where there's an American flag or a daily Pledge of Allegiance.  What are they going to do?  Take a knee in front of their desks or on an assembly line?  It would be ineffectual and downright silly.

But what does Trump care?  He got a lot of mileage out of it and distracted people from the Russia investigation.

## The Fictitious Wiretap of Trump Tower

No sooner was Trump in office when he started bad-mouthing President Obama at every turn and undoing every Obama policy that he could.

I don't have much to say about the claim by Trump that his building was wire-tapped under Obama, because it never really happened.

It's another case of the man who victimizes everybody trying to hide that fact by playing the victim.

## The Fictitiously Stolen 3,000,000 Votes in California

This never happened either.

## The Fictitiously Enormous Inauguration Crowd

Neither did this, and the photographs prove it.

## The "Witch Hunt" Against Trump

Trump keeps saying there was "NO COLLUSION" with Russia and that Robert Mueller's investigation is just a witch hunt, the most dreadful, evil conspiracy that anybody in the world has ever had to face.

But there have already been lots of guilty pleas and convictions of his campaign aides.

And he himself famously, or notoriously, cried out at one of his campaign rallies: "I will tell you this, Russia. If you're listening, I hope you're able to find the 30,000 emails that are missing. I think you will be mightily rewarded by our press."

Leon Panetta responded, "I find those kinds of statements to be totally outrageous because you've got now a presidential candidate who is, in fact, asking the Russians to engage in American politics. I just think that's beyond the pale."

Of course it is. But what does Trump care? Putin helped get him elected. In spirit, he's the *real* Manchurian Candidate, not Obama.

## Trump's Delusional Tweets

"My IQ is one of the highest -- and you all know it."

"I will be the best by far in fighting terror."

"I am the least racist person there is."

"Nobody but Donald Trump will save Israel."

"Nobody has more respect for women than Donald Trump."

"Nobody has done more for people with disabilities than me."

"Global warming is an expensive hoax!"

"Obama has no idea what he is doing -- incompetent."

"Obama has no problem lying to the American people."

"Mitt Romney is one of the dumbest and worst candidates in Republican history."

"Jeb Bush has no clue."

"I have long stated that Brian Williams was not a very smart guy."

"Jon Stewart a joke, not very bright and totally overrated."

"MSNBC's Lawrence O'Donnell dumbest political commentator on television...a face made for radio."

## The Enemy of the People

According to Donald Trump, the free press is "the enemy of the people."  It's the pot calling the kettle black.

Trump is the worst bully who ever occupied the Bully Pulpit. Instead of using it to encourage our better angels and uplift the nation, he spews out venom. His blind, hateful diatribes have put our entire society in danger, more danger than he might realize. I say this because I am reminded of Julius Streicher, publisher of the hate-mongering Nazi news-rag, *Der Sturmer*. During the Nuremberg trials, when he was confronted with the atrocities his bigotry had inspired, he said half-apologetically, "I never thought it would go this far."

Trump has the same problem when it comes to matters of conscience. Consider the five reporters who were gunned down in Baltimore. A more introspective person might wonder a little bit if it is possible that his hate talk played a subtle part in this tragedy. He vilifies the White House Press Corps and the entire Fourth Estate instead of regarding them as vital watchdogs of our democracy. He constantly calls reporters "horrible people, bad people," and encourages his supporters to despise them. He doesn't realize or doesn't care that this sets up just the right climate for some nut-case with a grudge to go over the edge and gun them down.

Concerned ahead of time that something like this might happen, CNN had said, "It is a sad day when the President of the United States encourages violence."

After it happened, Trump said, "Journalists, like all Americans, should be free from the fear of being violently attacked while doing their jobs."

If this isn't the height of hypocrisy, then what is?

# CHAPTER SEVENTEEN

## *The Tostito Acropolis*

I have been writing quite a bit about corporate greed, but what about corporate kitsch; i.e., tackiness?

In their lust to advertise themselves and their products in every possible way, with a complete lack of restraint and good taste, we now have to put up with their names and logos on things we never thought would succumb to such blatant exploitation:

The Tostito Sugar Bowl. Bank of America Field. Fedex Field. The Magic jack St. Petersburg Bowl. The Konica Minolta Gator Bowl. The Chick-fil-A Bowl. The Meineke Car Care Bowl. And on and on and on.

While I was listening to a Steelers-Colts game on my way back from a convention in Lexington, Kentucky, it struck me that our multinational corporations will probably not remain satisfied with plastering their names on stadium walls and gigantic electronic scoreboards. The game was being played in Lucas Oil Field, and it was coming to me from the Subway Broadcast Booth -- and I was hit with the marvelous realization that the Greeks could bail themselves out of their current financial difficulties by selling naming rights to their awe-inspiring national monuments!

In fact billions of dollars in naming-rights deals could save not only Greece but also many other financially strapped countries from impending bankruptcy and worldwide recession or even depression.

Donald Trump and his oligarchs would absolutely love it.

Here is my initial list of wonderful possibilities:

THE TOSTITO ACROPOLIS
THE KOCH BROTHERS PARTHENON
THE U.S. STEEL  SISTINE CHAPEL
THE WALMART WASHINGTON MONUMENT
THE K-MART GOLDEN GATE BRIDGE
THE ALCOA GETTYSBURG BATTLEFIELD
THE TOYOTA GREAT WALL OF CHINA
THE HONDA BIG BEN
THE HYUNDAI BUCKINGHAM PALACE
THE NISSAN HOLOCAUST MUSEUM
THE GETTY OIL LINCOLN MONUMENT

The list can go on and on. And as soon as this remarkable idea gets noticed by the president, it probably will.  But of course everything will have to be named after him, just like Trump Tower.  We can look forward to THE TRUMP PARTHENON.  THE TRUMP SISTINE CHAPEL.  THE TRUMP GREAT WALL OF CHINA. And so on.

Naming rights to classic movies also can be sold, and as trump acquires them we'll soon be watching:

THE TRUMP CASABLANCA
THE TRUMP CITIZEN KANE
THE TRUMP WIZARD OF OZ
THE TRUMP PSYCHO
THE TRUMP CHAINSAW MASSACRE
THE TRUMP GUNGA DIN
THE TRUMP NIGHT OF THE LIVING DEAD

I'm sure you will agree that the possibilities are endless and that he will surely be quick to seize on them. And he and his multinational corporations will continue to line their pockets in a big way while we continue to pay them for the demise of our democracy.

# PART FIVE

# SEX, VIOLENCE AND CENSORSHIP

Donald Trump isn't dealing wisely or effectively with any of the societal or cultural problems in this country; he's just divisively exaggerating and exasperating the problems to distract us from his own greed and possibly impeachable offenses.

Since I have long been troubled, in ways that he has not been, by the vital issues affecting this country, I have explored my deep concerns in a series of articles previously published in various formats.

These issues will not go away by being ignored, so once again I bring them forward, updated and expanded for this book.

-- John Russo

# CHAPTER EIGHTEEN

## *"Reel" Vs. Real Violence*

This article was first published in *Newsweek* and then republished in several college texts and anthologies. For weeks I was sought after as a guest on radio and TV stations across the nation in order to debate its thesis that the violence in America is not *caused* by the violence in movies but is a reflection of what we've caused to happen in real life, just as the gangsters and killers portrayed by James Cagney and Edward G. Robinson in the movies of the 1930's reflected what was going on in the bootleg era.

I was bombarded by threatening phone calls and hate mail. One lady said she wanted to spit in my face, and another one hoped I would die at the hands of one of the killers in my movies.

It was unnerving to get three heavy sacks of hate mail delivered to me by *Newsweek*. My article was meant as food for thought, not as an apology for every gory movie under the sun. But in any case, I now think that violent movies *are* actually part of the problem. And not just horror movies, of which I have made many. I think that movies like *Dirty Harry* and *The Terminator* and so forth are far worse than my movie *Midnight,* for example, because they are *reality-based*, not *fantasy*, and they seem to push the notion that if somebody pisses you off you should just shoot them.

Here is *"Reel" Vs. Real violence*, first published in 1990:


One day I switched on the evening news just in time to see a Pennsylvania politician waving around a .357 magnum, warning reporters to back off so they wouldn't get hurt, then sticking the gun in his mouth and...

Mercifully, the station I was watching didn't show him pulling the trigger, but I learned later that another Pittsburgh station showed the whole suicide unedited. What I saw was enough to make me ill. My stomach was in a knot, and I couldn't get the incident out of my mind. I still can't, even though a number of years have gone by.

I have a special reason for wondering and worrying about blood and violence on TV and movie screens. I write, produce and direct horror movies. I co-authored *Night of the Living Dead*, the so-called "granddaddy of the splatter flicks." And since then I've made a string of murders depicting murder and mayhem.

I can watch these kinds of movies when they've been made by other people, and I can even help create the bloody effects in my own movies without getting a knot in my stomach. Yet I still retain my capacity to be shocked, horrified and saddened when something like this happens in real life.

So there must be a difference between real violence and "reel" violence. And if I didn't feel that this is true, I'd stop making the kinds of movies I make. What are those differences?

My movies are scary and unsettling, but they are also cautionary tales. They might show witches at work, doing horrible things or carrying out nefarious schemes, but in doing so they convey a warning against superstition and the dementia it can spawn. They might show people under extreme duress, set upon by human or inhuman creatures, but in doing so they teach people how duress can be handled and how blind, ignorant fear can be confronted and conquered. My purpose hasn't been to glorify and encourage murder and mayhem, but to give horror fans the vicarious chills and thrills that they crave.

The most powerful and, consequently, financially successful horror movies -- *Night of the Living Dead, The Texas Chainsaw Massacre, Halloween* and *Friday the 13th* -- feature a small cast in a confined situation that is made terrifying by the presence of a monster/madman/murderer. Usually the victims are young, beautiful women. Often the murders are filmed from the point of view of the murderer. For all these reasons, we filmmakers have been accused of hating women and portraying them as objects to be punished for being sexually desirable. Horror fans have been accused of identifying with the psychopathic killers portrayed in these movies and deriving vicarious enjoyment from watching the killers act out the fans' dark fantasies.

But there are two simple, pragmatic reasons why the victims are often filmed from the point of view of the killer. First, it's an effective technique for not revealing who the killer is, thus preserving an aura of suspense. Secondly, it affords dramatically explicit angles for showing the victim's terror -- and the horror of what the killer is doing.

These films *are* horrifying because they reflect -- but do not create -- a frightful trend in our society. Murders, assaults and rapes are being committed with more frequency and with increasing brutality. Serial killers and mass murderers are constantly making headlines. Most of these killers are men, often sexually warped men, and they most often kill women. So we filmmakers have stuck to the facts in our portrayals of them. That's why our movies are so scary. Too many of our fellow citizens are turning into monsters, and contemporary horror movies have seized upon this fear and personified it. So now we have Jason, Michael and Freddy instead of Dracula and Frankenstein. Our old-time movie monsters used to be creatures of fantasy. But today, unfortunately, they are extensions of reality.

Recently, at a horror convention in Albany, I was autographing videocassettes of a show I had hosted entitled *Witches, Vampires and Zombies,* and a young man asked me if the tape showed actual human sacrifices. He was disappointed when I informed him that the ceremonies on the tape were fictional depictions. He was looking for "snuff movies" -- the kind that actually show people dying.

Unfortunately, tapes showing real death are widely available nowadays. A video of the Pennsylvania politician blowing his brains out went on sale just a few weeks after the incident was broadcast. But I don't think that the people who are morbidly fixated on this sort of thing are the same people who are in love with the horror-movie genre.

I'm afraid that the young man I met in Albany has a serious personality disorder. And I don't think he's really a horror fan. He didn't buy my tape, but he would have, if the human sacrifices had been real.  "Reel" violence didn't interest him.  He didn't care about the niceties of theme, plot or character development.  He just wanted to see people die.

I haven't seen any snuff movies for sale at the horror conventions I've attended.  True horror fans aren't interested.  They don't go to the movies just to see artificial blood and gore, either.  The films that gratuitously deliver those kinds of effects usually are box-office flops.  The hit horror films have a lot more to offer.  While scaring us and entertaining us, they teach us how to deal with our deepest fears, dreads and anxieties.

But modern horror movies aren't to blame for these fears, dreads and anxieties.  They didn't create our real-life Jasons, Michaels and Freddys any more than the gangster movies of the 1920's and 1930's created Al Capone and Dutch Schultz. If the movies reflect, with disturbing accuracy, the psychic terrain of the world we live in, then it's up to us to change that world and make it a safer place.

# CHAPTER NINETEEN

*Angels and Demons*

One day in 1999 on the evening news I learned of the apparent mass suicide of thirty-nine young members of a religious cult at a mansion they had rented in San Diego. They were found lying on beds, cots and mattresses, their arms at their sides, as if they had fallen asleep. They were all wearing black trousers and tennis shoes. Each had a purple shroud over his or her head.

As I drove toward my office the following day, a report on the radio said that the members of this cult believed they were angels sent to earth to usher in an era of peace. They did not drink or smoke, and were celibate. They ranged in age from 18 to 24, which is considered the prime age for cult recruitment.

I have long been intrigued and horrified by the dangers and the evils of perverted religious beliefs and superstitions, and in my fiction I have explored this theme in considerable depth. Here, for example, are two quotes from the front of my novel *Hell's Creation*:

"Satan is a symbol, nothing more. He's a symbol of man's carnal nature -- his lust, greed, vengeance, but most of all his ego."

"The thing that distinguishes man from the other animals, more than any other factor, is his ability to sublimate. His highly developed intellect can and does override his instincts. This has produced some of his noblest achievements and basest perversions."

The first quote is from Anton La Vey, a self-styled modern-day witch. The second quote was made up by me and put into the mouth of one of my more striking characters, Dr. Morgan Drey, an anthropologist appalled by people's belief in devils. In his imaginary book, *The Appeal of Witchcraft*, Dr. Drey goes on to say:

"It is no accident that the devil is portrayed in medieval woodcuts as a cloven-hoofed beast with his tongue in the shape of a triple penis. Sadism is a sexual perversion. And a belief in witchcraft is the horrid sickness of a sexually repressed society. Religious fanaticism gives birth to witchcraft by encouraging a deep-rooted fear of a supposed very real devil who walks the earth with an assortment of demons who may possess living persons."

My fictional character, Dr. Morgan Drey, might also have pointed out that a feeling of powerlessness, as well as sexual repression, can fuel superstitious beliefs. In medieval times, people had little understanding or control over their environment; a belief in spells, potions, demons, witches and angels created the illusion of some power and some understanding.

Today's cults, whether the members believe they are devils or angels, purport to fill a similar intellectual and emotional void. The thirty-nine young people in San Diego were probably highly sensitive to the uncertainties, ambiguities and outright horrors of modern society, and came to believe that they were the "angels" sent to earth to make things right.  This week, Easter week, was their Holy Week.  I assume they thought that if they died, if they sacrificed themselves for the good of the world, they would ascend into Heaven.  According to cult expert Mike Kropveid, quoted in *USA Today*, members of cults are often characterized by "magical thinking, the belief that when things get tough, thcrc's some secret formula out there for instant nirvana.  In their perspective, they do not commit suicide, but decide to depart and go into another plane of existence."

As I said in an article I wrote for *Newsweek*, I consider my horror novels to be cautionary tales -- warnings in fictionalized form of the dangers that can be perpetrated by the human mind when it succumbs to delusions.  And these delusions, these twisted beliefs, can weave themselves into the framework of foolish superstition, pseudo-religion, or even misguided science.

Horror fans are by and large very gentle people who enjoy the vicarious thrills offered by books and movies, but would be appalled at the idea of facing a real serial killer or trying to behave like one.

We live in a brutal society.  But even when our society was less brutal, horror films and murder stories were extremely popular because they deal with the most powerful, most highly dramatic human situations and emotions.

Edgar Allan Poe believed that there was no richer or more powerful subject for fiction than the death of a beautiful woman.  Historically, horror movies have revolved around beautiful, innocent women being pursued by monsters, from Faye Wray in *King Kong* to Jamie Lee

Curtis in *Halloween*. These films do not encourage murder. On the contrary, the horror in horror movies comes from the fact that the viewer *doesn't want* anything bad to happen to the heroine and roots for her to overcome and destroy whatever evil might be pursuing her.

I know that the modern world is a scary, dangerous place. I hate to see women or men or children abused, raped or murdered. But I don't hate horror movies. They're not the main problem.

From *Oedipus Rex* to *Hamlet* to *The Silence of the Lambs* and beyond, dramatists have exploited the public's fascination with the dark side of human nature. This is as it should be. The human race will never learn to cope with its tendency toward self-destruction until it understands and controls its darkest impulses. The novelist, the filmmaker, help us to cast a bright light on those impulses and flush them out into the open.

*Hamlet* and *Oedipus Rex* both dealt with incestuous relationships, sexual jealousy and violated sexual taboos that led to murder and suicide. *The Silence of the Lambs* dealt with a warped sexuality that produced a demented personality and led to a string of horrible killings.

The value of these works, beyond their ability to intrigue and entertain, is their ability to help us understand human nature in its worst manifestations, so that its best manifestations might be encouraged and enhanced. And, knowing that we will not always succeed in this, to at least teach us how to be cautious, lest we fall victim to the demented ones who prowl among us, always looking to fool us and disarm our suspicions to make us discard our self-protective instincts.

What were the roots of my own particular fascination with the dark side of human nature?  I can trace it back to a day when at age thirteen, I found a copy of *Police Gazette* magazine hidden under my father's workbench.  It contained a lengthy article on Ed Gein, the ghoulish real-life serial killer who became the inspiration for many novels and movies, including *Psycho, Deranged* and *The Texas Chainsaw Massacre*.  I was repulsed and yet intrigued by the true-crime story that I read in the *Police Gazette*.  The real Ed Gein was a homicidal transvestite who killed his mother and made a vest out of her  breasts and wore them around the house.  Years later, this lurid detail was to become a key element in *The Silence of the Lambs*.

Ever since reading that article about Gein, I've been fascinated with the psychology behind serial killers -- not only Ed Gein but also Ted Bundy, Jeffrey Dahmer, Wayne Gacey, and on and on and on.  It appalls me that 75% of the world's serial killers live in America.  Why?  How did they get that way?  What is it that caused their sexual impulses to become twisted toward violence?  I don't know if we will ever fully understand these things. But we've got to try, in the hope that a deeper understanding might lead to prevention.

What we do know is that repressed sexuality, warped sexuality, often seeks an outlet in violence.  The centers of the human brain that have to do with sex and violence are very close together anatomically.  Perhaps, metaphorically speaking, the wires can too easily become crossed, short-circuiting and producing a deformed personality.

I've made a study of these deformed personalities -- serial killers -- and portrayed them in fictional form in my books and movies.  I've pointed out that they are the monsters of our time.  In portraying their tendency to rape and kill beautiful young women, novelists and filmmakers are telling the truth about them -- that they do mostly go after young women, and that thought is as appalling and frightening to us filmmakers as it is to the young women and men who buy most of our scary books and movies.

Many people are running scared these days.  They see the high crime rate (which has actually been going down lately, although Donald Trump pretends that it isn't) and the deteriorating quality of their lives (caused by the milking and abuse of the middle class and the poor), and they want to run and hide -- or, worse, take out their aggressions on others.  For instance, they buy into Trump's constant blaming of the crime rate on immigrants; he's all too willing to hang dreadful labels on anybody "different."  Irrational fear makes people look for boogey-men everywhere. But the real evil is the narrow-mindedness that throughout history has spawned the worst kind of perversion and has led to epidemics of sadistic violence and persecution of millions of innocent people.

Theology and religion mixed with politics can go horribly wrong in the hands of fascists.  That is the mentality that burns crosses, desecrates synagogues, guns down patients and doctors in abortion clinics, bombs government buildings and assassinates civil rights leaders.

Religious fanatics believe that they are acting "in the service of God."  We have to always remember that when their ilk held almost absolute power, they wanted to burn Copernicus at the stake for proving that the earth revolved around the sun.  In their "Holy Wisdom" they believed the opposite; their minds were made up and they didn't want to be confused by facts.  During the Inquisition, they were more than willing to exterminate millions by hanging them or burning them at the stake, in order to hang onto their false beliefs and maintain their hold over others.

Our Founding Fathers learned well the lessons of history.  They gave us a republic and a United States Constitution that strives to preserve the separation of church and state, so that our government will not be able to impose any particular religious system on everybody.

But many people, regrettably, including the current occupant of the White House, don't understand or appreciate what the Constitution is all about.  They think that their way is the one true way, and they don't mind using political or economic means to force it upon us all.

The Hard Right Christians want to see a theocracy ruling not just the United States but the entire world, even if it takes the End of Days to bring it on, with Jesus Christ as dictator.  The Hard Right Muslims are no better, but they want it to be Allah.

What does Trump care?  As long as he gets their votes.

# CHAPTER TWENTY

*Fear and Superstition*

We are living in a nation gripped by fear.

Nothing new about that, you might say. During World War Two we feared attack by the Germans and the Japanese. And during the Cold War we built concrete bomb shelters and made school children practice hiding under their desks in case the Russians or the Chinese hit us with nuclear warheads.

But at least those fears were centered around a real or potentially real foreign threat.

These days we live in fear of ourselves.

Home-grown criminals rape, rob, stab and shoot at us at an epidemic rate. Home-grown terrorists blow us up with homemade bombs made out of fertilizer.

We are afraid of love, afraid of romance, afraid of sex, afraid of herpes and, even now, still afraid of AIDS.

Popular music is increasingly unromantic, angry and cruel. Sometimes it helps incite the violence that we perpetuate against ourselves.

We are afraid of what we have become. We lament the innocence we have lost. And we feel an urge to travel backwards to try to recapture a sense of innocence.

Our search for simplistic solutions causes some of us to behave like ignorant, superstitious primitives, not knowing whether to run from the fire, the lightning or the thunder -- or pray to it.

Some parents in my neighborhood are so afraid of modern life that they have chosen to withdraw from it by joining a "fundamentalist" religious sect that requires their children to be taken out of the public schools and taught at home so that their minds can be "kept clean."

Many kinds of sex are so taboo to them that they don't want their children to have any kind of sex education at all.  Since they are afraid of "godless science," they don't want their children to learn about evolution.  They forbid dancing and dating and the wearing of shorts and low-cut dresses.  They don't permit their children to go trick-or-treating on Halloween, because they regard that holiday as pagan "devil worship."

Back in the Dark Ages, All Hallows Eve was thought to be a night when ghosts, demons and goblins walked the land.  Is that where we're headed?  Is our fear of each other driving us back into the Dark Ages?

I think that until we learn to laugh at our ancient superstitions, we shall never be free of them.  Until we learn who we are and where we came from -- including how we evolved from more primitive creatures -- we are not going to fully understand ourselves, with all our faults and all our virtues.  Until we learn to face modern problems instead of hiding from them, our dread and terror will only grow worse.

We need to keep reaching out to each other, and keep reaching out for knowledge.  That's what separates us from our savage ancestors -- and our savage contemporaries. In the absence of knowledge and understanding, and without the willingness to keep on inquiring and learning, we revert to mindless, helpless ignorance that makes us fear the lightning and the thunder, the dangers of the perilous and marvelous world we live in, and the hopes and dreams of other people, more like us than different from us, who are coming here in search of a better life.

# CHAPTER TWENTY-ONE

## *The Fate of the Pick-Axe Killer*

I wrote this article right after Karla Faye Tucker was executed by lethal injection.  Her fate was a raging issue for years before it was finally decided, and I was motivated to write about it:

Last week Karla Faye Tucker was executed in spite of the best efforts of her lawyers and supporters, including Geraldo Rivera, Charles Grodin, Reverend Pat Robertson and Pope John Paul.  My personal philosophy and my views on social and ethical issues are quite often at odds with those of  Rivera, the Reverend and the Pope, but I usually find that Charles Grodin and I are on the same wavelength, but this time that's not exactly the case.·

Try as I might, I could not make myself believe that Karla Faye's life should be spared.  Fourteen years ago, she killed her lover and *his* lover with a pick-axe. She drove the heavy spiked tool into each of their bodies at least thirty times, and said that she had an orgasm with each blow.  Her female victim at first begged for mercy, but then started begging to be killed because the pain was so bad.  But Karla Faye showed no mercy.

In prison, the "pick-axe killer" experienced a religious conversion, and became "born again."  She claimed to no longer be the same person who had committed those heinous murders.  Well, I say that she *was* the same person.  Her views may have changed, her personality may have changed, but that does not mean that she could have  or should have evaded responsibility for her own actions.

If she was truly enlightened, truly remorseful, for the heinous acts she committed, she should have willingly gone to her death.  I know that I could not live with myself if I had done anything like that.  Nor would I deserve to.

I would have believed more strongly in the "new" Karla Faye if she had instructed her lawyers to end her appeals and speed up her execution.  Instead she became a media centerpiece for the endless debate over capital punishment and whether or not it is a deterrent.

Well, I *know* that it is.  Let me tell you why.

I'll never forget the day, back in the late forties or early fifties, when all the kids on our block went to see a Saturday matinee of *Angels with Dirty Faces*.  James Cagney played a tough, charismatic gangster who was idolized by Leo Gorcey and the Dead End Kids.  Finally convicted of murder, he vows to go to the electric chair bravely, without a whimper.  But the priest in the movie, played by Pat O'Brien, is fighting an uphill battle for these kids' hearts, minds and souls.  He visits Cagney on Death Row and begs him to, in effect, die like a coward, so the kids might turn away from a similar life of crime and not end just as tragically.  But Cagney refuses.

This all leads up to the big climactic moment when

Cagney is escorted out of his death cell and made to walk "the last mile."  The electric chair with its straps and hood beckons ominously, dreadfully, at the end of a long semi-dark corridor.

And Cagney does finally crack.

He has to be dragged, screaming and bawling, to be slammed down and strapped into that chair.

The hood is pulled over his face, and while the priest prays the switch is pulled.

That scene had a profound, terrifying effect on me and all the other kids on my block.  After seeing the movie, we huddled together, sitting on the curb, and we all said that we never wanted to do anything in our whole lives that would cause us to have to go to the electric chair.

That movie made punishment and retribution seem swift, terrible and sure.  I don't actually know whether or not people on Death Row in those days lingered for years and years like they do today.  But my point is that we kids didn't think about that.  The mere fact that the electric chair was out there waiting for us, if we did anything to deserve it, was enough to help scare us onto "the straight and narrow."

The deterrent effect of what happened to Karla Faye Tucker may have been lessened by the fourteen years it took to bring her to her fate, but it was a fate that she set in motion by her own reprehensible actions.  Those who would forgive her point out that she was led into prostitution and drug addiction at a tender age by her own mother.  This is, of course, a sad and woeful mitigating factor that was considered in heartfelt agony by the judge, the jury, the governor and Supreme Court, who apparently decided, as I did, that we must have a society that tells people that, no matter how angry or mistreated you may feel over your lot in life, you *must not* take the life of another human being.

NOTE:  Some years after I wrote this article, as a result of my continuing interest in the crime of murder and how justice is served or not served, I have over and over again seen that killers do *not* want to be killed.  They will make just about any deal that sends them to Death Row, where there remains some hope of eventual freedom (or at least a continuing life among the living, even if in a ten-by-ten cell), if the deal spares them from a death sentence.

This threat of being put to death is a valuable tool for police and prosecutors.  They use it to get confessions, sometimes for murders they didn't even know about or couldn't prove, and at other times they get the murderer to tell where the body or bodies of their victims are so that the remains can be returned to suffering friends and family for a proper burial.

So what I am saying is that one benefit of capital punishment that few people ever mention is that it helps the police to get murderers off our streets.  That is an advantage that I would not like to give up.

# CHAPTER TWENTY-TWO

*The Selling of O.J.*

In the mid-nineties I became unexpectedly involved with the hoopla surrounding what was called the Murder Case of the Century: the murders of Nicole Simpson and Ron Goldman, for which television celebrity O.J. Simpson was charged and put on trial.

I got involved with the hoopla, not the trial, but I watched the trial for hours, whenever I could, because I was so keenly interested in the outcome. When you are a public person, like I am, and when you work in the media and entertainment field, as I do, many unlikely involvements come your way. The O.J. Simpson murders were one of the top examples of this, and my part in the aftermath happened because my friends George Romero and Bill Hinzman made a sports documentary about Simpson back when he was just about the biggest star of all the star athletes in the United States.

When the murders happened, people were clamoring to know more about him, including his past.

I'm the person who sold clips of *Juice on the Loose*, a 47-minute biographical film that was in large measure a puff piece, to 20/20, *Hard Copy*, *Inside Edition*, and just about every other big-time news outlet you can think of.  I also negotiated the deal with Vidmark Entertainment that resulted in national distribution of Romero's film about O.J. on home video and elsewhere.

When George Romero heard that I was the agent for these deals, he phoned me complaining that I was, in his words, "exploiting O.J."

I said, "Well, what were you doing when you shot the film in the first place?  He's almost certainly guilty, and this film is a valuable social document.  Ph.D. candidates are going to be writing theses about it years from now."

He said, "You're exploiting O.J.  I'm going to go on TV and denounce it."

And he did just that.

Looking back on George's challenge, I realize that he was just as reluctant, or rather more reluctant, to believe in Simpson's guilt than I was.  Like everyone else, we had bought into the image we had repeatedly seen on television of O.J. the hero running through an airport with armloads of luggage, or of O.J. breaking the rushing record by going over the 2,000-yeard barrier for the first time in sports history.

Legendary broadcaster Howard Cosell was calling him "the perfect athlete."  So charming, so charismatic, so anxious to please!

Television makes stars out of talented persons or even lesser talents.  The image makers get us to confuse the images with reality.  This, in large measure, is the phenomenon behind Arnold Schwarzenegger, Ronald Reagan and Donald Trump.  We believe what we see.  We think we know them because of the images, the likeability that has charmed us over and over again when they come into our homes, on TV.

Maybe we ought to think twice before ever voting again for someone we've seen on television.

Anyway, these are some of my current thoughts on the subject, but back then I was primarily focused on making deals. How the deals were negotiated in a flurry of wheeling and dealing over a three-week binge of 18- to 20-hour days, is a valuable lesson for anybody who might make a feature movie, a documentary, or any other type of film that suddenly finds itself in the center of a media frenzy. I had a fast and furious bidding war going on over *Juice on the Loose*. But even so, one of the key things I found out was that the sums commonly believed to be paid by the TV news magazine shows are grossly exaggerated in the minds of the public. We took in quite a bit of money -- but nothing like the millions that were initially envisioned.

When I say "we" I refer to my partners, Bill Hinzman and Hal Priore. We had all known and worked with each other for a long time, and our involvement with the O.J. Simpson film and the package of sports documentaries of which it was a part, went back more than twenty years. There were fourteen sports documentaries in what was called *The Winners* series, centering around such stars as Willie Stargell, O.J. Simpson, Kareem Abdul Jabbar, Mario Andretti, Bruno Sammartino, Lou Brock, and so on.

The Willie Stargell film which I already mentioned in a previous chapter, was entitled *What if I wasn't a Ballplayer?* and was produced by Hal Priore back in 1970 when I was still at George Romero's company, The Latent Image, Inc.,  I worked on the Stargell movie but then I left to form my own company, and did not work on any of the other movies in *The Winners* series.  Bill Hinzman was hired to replace me, and so he worked on all the remaining thirteen films.  He buddied around with O.J. and his football pals Al Cowlings and Joe Bell, and filmed O.J.'s mother, father, brothers, sisters and first wife, plus his children Arnelle and Justin, over the long weeks of making the documentary.

In the mid-eighties, after The Latent Image folded, Bill Hinzman and Hal Priore obtained the rights to *The Winners* movies, and in 1994  they hired me, through my company Market Square Productions, Inc., to remarket them.  We were getting ready to do just that when Nicole Simpson and Ron Goldman were murdered.  And this suddenly made *Juice on the Loose* much more valuable than any of the other thirteen.  Bill and Hal wanted me to agent it, and I sprang to it, knowing that *timeliness* was crucial.  In the first few days or weeks following the murders and O.J.'s arrest, the media would be wild to dig up footage pertaining to the older, happier, glory days of his career, but as the story moved on, that stuff would be shoved right out of the headlines by hot, fast-breaking developments.  So, whatever I was going to sell, I had to sell it *now!*

The first thing I did was screen *Juice on the Loose* so I could write a synopsis that would stimulate various buyers.  As I said before, to me the film was a valuable social document, offering tantalizing insights into the psyche of a sports hero who seemingly had a dark side that had toppled him from his lofty pedestal.

As a novelist and filmmaker whose work often focuses on bizarre murders and the pathology behind them, I will reiterate that I was keenly interested in the Simpson case from the beginning. I tossed and turned, losing sleep for many nights after news hit about the murders, finding it hard to believe that O.J. committed them and hoping against hope that somehow he'd turn out not to be guilty. I never met him personally, but like a majority of Americans I was charmed by his public image and I hated to think that someone so likeable, with "everything going for him," might turn out to have done something so terrible.

In the film O.J. says, "I always had an ego, had to stand out, had to be a leader. Football is my vehicle to come out of the ghetto. I need recognition, friendship, lots of friendship. I have a need to be known, to be recognized."

Star Buffalo Bills lineman Reggie McKenzie, the blocker who's credited with helping to make O.J. a star, says, "If O.J. lost everything he could pick hisself up and go on. He'll be a legend. I'll be able to tell my grandchildren I was with O.J. I'll always have that to remember."

O.J.'s last lines are, "When O.J. dies everybody's gonna be talking about him." Those lines are of course much more prophetic and ironic that he would have thought.

After reviewing the film, I wrote, "In light of the present tragedy that has stunned the world and absorbed our attention, this documentary reverberates with pathos, nostalgia and glimmerings of insight into how a charismatic sports hero, who seemed to have everything the American Dream can offer, ultimately descended into a nightmare."

While Bill Hinzman was making numerous dubs of the movie, I was on the phone making calls to every TV show and home video distributor that might possibly be interested. I also was faxing and mailing the synopsis, with a package of press clippings, to all the potential buyers.

As I said, I got a bidding war going. TV programs were all fired up and most wanted an exclusive right to use clips for a specified period. Our heads filled with stories about huge amounts of money paid for hot, newsworthy material, and we didn't want to start out asking too low a price and have to settle for it. Friends and entertainment-business associates were already telling us we were going to get rich, their voices loaded with admiration and envy. After some discussion, Bill, Hal and I decided to start off asking $50,000 for clips. We figured we might get laughed at, but if we didn't come out of the gate with a high price tag, we'd never know whether or not we could have scored big.

The $50,000 figure was laughed at by everybody, but I didn't mind. I was not embarrassed. I was beginning to learn what the market would bear. Although I had been in the entertainment business for thirty years, writing, producing and directing -- and then selling or helping to sell -- hundreds of productions from TV commercials on up to theatrical features, I had never before had occasion to sell any of my movies to TV news shows. I had never owned or agented anything that was hot in that particular way.

As it turned out, even though they were clamoring for our material, *Hard Copy* offered only $5,000 for three minutes' worth of clips, plus $1,000 for each additional minute to be used in succeeding weeks. *Inside Edition* offered $8,500 for three-and-a-half minutes of clips, $1,500 for an additional one-minute clip, plus $2,000 per minute for any clips used after that. It all sounds very simple and straight-forward the way I've condensed it for this article, but to arrive at this point I spent days and nights running around like mad, going from phone to fax machine to copy machine, with lots of errands and meetings in between, and cramming take-out meals into my mouth while I wheeled and dealt.

At first the main bidding battle was between *Hard Copy* and *Inside Edition*. They kept upping each other's ante and pleading for exclusivity. But then ABC came into the picture. The other two had said in no uncertain terms that they would beat any offer that ABC made. And so I got back to them when ABC offered $20,000 for twenty minutes' worth of clips. And they both promptly folded.

I said, "What happened to your claim that you'd beat any offer ABC made?" And I was told that $20,000 was out of the question.

I was therefore confident that I had succeeded in my mission of selling the clips for no less than what the market would bear.

Meantime I landed a deal for video distribution by Vidmark, for a $30,000 advance against 15% of the profits. The other video distributors folded. Most of them were set up in such a way that they required six to nine months of in-house preparation to put out a program. And by that time, they felt, interest in O.J. Simpson would have progressed beyond the early biographical material and on to current developments and revelations concerning the murders.

We entertained high hopes for cassette sales and royalties, but they did not materialize. Public interest, as predicted, progressed very quickly beyond what we had to offer. It also seemed to me that many people, feeling that O.J. was guilty, didn't want to buy anything that might show him in a positive light.

As for me, I was so angry when he didn't get convicted, that I gave up all my rights in *Juice on the Loose.* I didn't want to make another penny off of a person that I believed should have gone to prison.

But I still believe that the film needs to be seen by anyone interested, not just in whether or not O.J. is guilty of the murders, but in the way that star athletes and other celebrities are placed on pedestals in our society. As we have seen with O.J. Simpson, Matt Bauer, Bill Cosby, Roman Polanski, Robert Blake, Phil Spector, and to a large extent Donald Trump, their public images can have scant relationship to the reality of their personal defects, and those contrived images can often enable them to pull the wool over our eyes and effectively insulate them from the consequences of their actions.

# PART SIX

# SEND A ZOMBIE TO CONGRESS

It's time for a laugh break with some sharp-witted satire! The articles in Part Six were written during President Obama's first election campaign, but many of the points made in them still apply, or will at least give us a nostalgic look back to when we had a smart, decent, sophisticated president.

Back in those "Good Old Days" not so long ago but seeming a lifetime away from us now, Russ Streiner and I launched a web site called SEND A ZOMBIE TO CONGRESS. It was of course tongue-in-cheek, but carried the implication that, dumb brutes that the zombies are, they might be preferable to the greedy dunderheads who are still there, sent back year after year to gorge themselves at our expense.

# CHAPTER TWENTY-THREE

*What is "Send a Zombie to Congress"?*

We are John Russo and Russ Streiner, the screenwriter and producer of *Night of the Living Dead.*

We created *Send a Zombie to Congress* because we, along with some of our friends and fans, have been impelled to lend our support to the presidential campaign of Barack Obama.

Why?

Because we could no longer sit silently on the sidelines listening to the lies and distortions of the opposing campaign. We have young people in our families and young people in the movie making program that we teach, and this presidential election is of monumental importance to every one of them. They represent the future of our democracy. And we want it to survive and flourish.

The destruction of the principles of our Constitution and the mishandling of our government by Bush and his right-wing cohorts must be rejected. Their greed, fear-mongering and wrong-headed policies have led to bankruptcies, foreclosures, trillion-dollar bail-outs, collapsing infrastructure and endless, unnecessary war.

Yet they want to be rewarded with four more years.

Four more years in which to load our Supreme Court with justices who will overturn Roe v. Wade and bring us ever closer to the kind of narrow-minded, repressive, Big Brother brand of government that our Founding Fathers feared and deplored.

*Send a Zombie to Congress* is an attention-getting metaphor for a grassroots endeavor with a vital underlying purpose. We must band together to rescue our democracy. Our government is not working for "we the people," and Barack Obama represents our hope for change.

Please help us send Barack Obama to the White House.

We sincerely hope you will join us in this patriotic effort.

# CHAPTER TWENTY-FOUR

*Zombies have Wisely entered Politics!*

Who woulda thunk it? The flesh-eating ghouls depicted in the classic horror movie *Night of the Living Dead* are no longer the simple-minded critters we first came to know and love back in the sixties.

To our astonishment, they have now taken a decisive hand in the presidential election of 2008! And they're backing Barack Obama!

This shows they're not really stupid, they're not really brain dead, in fact they're a lot smarter than many living people out there who put zombies down and consider themselves superior.

Tired of being mocked, tired of seeing the country go to hell in a hand basket because of the brain-dead policies of the George Bush presidency, the zombies are going after the fat-cats who aided and abetted his colossal blunders. From now on, until Barack Obama is righteously elected, they have vowed to dine only on the flesh of these greedy, self-serving hypocritical lobbyists and legislators.

Some insensitive cultural analysts and talking heads

have expressed befuddlement over their belated realization that flesh-eating zombies are actually capable of making intelligent choices when it comes to national elections. But they should've wised up to this fact before now-- the clues were always there for the observant among us.

My friend George Romero liked to explore the evolution of zombies into intelligent beings.  In *Night of the Living Dead* it was clear that they could wield crude weapons such as clubs and rocks.  Later, in *Dawn of the Dead*, they were already behaving a lot like us.  And in *Land of the Dead* one of them was fooling around with a trombone and trying to remember how to play it!

Nowadays the evolution is rather complete, and while not yet perfect, the steps taken so far must be applauded.

If these zombies' rotting hearts are in the right place, shouldn't yours be?  Shouldn't you be helping them in their attempt to help you by using the only means they know to get the fat-cats out of Washington?

Vote for Barack Obama and Joe Biden.  Fill both houses of Congress with liberal Democrats.

This time Washington *really* needs a change!  And even the (brain dead?) zombies know it!

So *Send a Zombie to Congress* -- where he or she can find something really good to chomp on!

# CHAPTER TWENTY-FIVE

*Zombies form Political Action Committee!*

They're truly not as brain dead as formerly believed!

The flesh-eating zombies first documented in *Night of the Living Dead* have evolved into political junkies determined to have an impact on the 2008 elections. To channel their energies into a proper direction, producer Russ Streiner and writer John Russo have helped them form their own ad hoc advocacy group under the banner *Send a Zombie to Congress*.

"These modern zombies aren't as brain damaged as you might imagine," Streiner enthused. "Indeed they have some very good ideas. They want to eliminate the fat-cats in Washington, and they want to help elect Barack Obama. You don't have to be a zombie to believe as they do."

Russo adds, "You also don't have to be a zombie to join our PAC. Check out our web site. There are lots of things zombies can't do on their own. Their rotting hearts are in the right place, but they desperately need the help of average Americans."

Asked by this somewhat worried reporter exactly how their horde of zombies would seek to "eliminate the fat-cats," Russo and Streiner were evasive.  Russo parried the question, stating only that the flesh-eaters were justifiably upset with the wrongheaded policies of the past eight years and wanted to do something about them "in their own way."

"This time Washington *really* needs a change," Streiner said, "and even the brain-dead zombies know it."

# CHAPTER TWENTY-SIX

*Zombie PAC Vows to Fight on!*

The Zombie Political Action Committee headed by John Russo and Russ Streiner issued an ominous policy statement that will have newly elected officials quaking in their boots for years to come.

"The collapse of our economy, the depletion of our military, and the destruction of the middle class didn't happen overnight," Streiner said. "It took years of stupidity and greed. And we're going to make sure it doesn't happen again."

"This time these fat-cats can't sit back and cool it just because they managed to get elected," Russo added. "If that happens, we won't be able to restrain our constituents."

By "constituents" Russo clearly means the horde of zombies he and Streiner control -- but just barely. Shaking his head sadly but ominously, he said, "If this new Congress fails to deliver the real and meaningful changes this country needs, we can't be held responsible for the terrible consequences. Zombies have to eat, and they've taken a liking to fat-cats, especially those who lie and don't keep their promises."

Asked for his own explanation as to why these zombies, previously believed to be brain dead, have suddenly taken such a strong interest in national politics, Mr. Streiner said, "We think they still have some functioning synapses, and these mostly inert parts of their mentality are greatly stimulated by outrage. Outrage over the wrong-headed policies and outright corruption that have dismantled our Constitution and severely threatened the lifelines of our democracy."

"The Founding Fathers would be turning over in their graves," Russo said, seemingly unaware of the irony. "If they came back today, they'd definitely approve of what we and our constituents are doing. In fact they'd probably hasten to join us."

# CHAPTER TWENTY-SEVEN

*Obama's Rope-a-Dope*

President Obama has made his enemies pay a stiff price for underestimating his wit, intelligence and acute sense of political timing and strategy.

NOTE: "Rope-a-Dope" was a term coined by boxer Muhammad Ali to describe how he would cover up and play "hurt" while waiting for an opportunity to deliver a match-ending counter-punch.

Obama rope-a-doped politically for over two years, often letting himself appear weak in the eyes of pundits, opponents and even his own worried and fidgety base, which was the risk he had to take in order to fully expose the "Party of No" and back them into a corner.  As a result of this clever but risky gambit, it has become excruciatingly clear to most voters that these congressional hypocrites have been willing to take this country to the brink of economic disaster for the poor and middle class, just so long as they and their wealthiest supporters can hang onto their grossly unfair share of wealth, power and tax cuts.

We see now how President Obama has outwitted

them.  He lulled them to sleep, then struck back hard, with enough time left to consolidate his gains before the 2012 elections.  All along, while he endured the skepticism and disappointment in the eyes of many, his own eyes remained diligently focused on an endgame of winner take all in which he was always betting on himself to be the ultimate winner.

He had to keep on being "the adult in the room" while swallowing pills that were bitter, not just for him but for his erstwhile supporters and admirers.  He had to endure their disappointment and disenchantment.  They wanted him to be bolder, to stand up and fight even when he understood that he would probably have been kayoed.  They said he was a poor negotiator, that he gave up too much even before talks were started.  They said he should have fought harder for a single-payer health care system.  They said he shouldn't have given up so much to Wall Street.  They said he shouldn't have let the Bush tax cuts stay in place -- even when it was the price he (and all of us) had to pay in order to prevent America from defaulting on its debts for the first time in history.

It is clear to most people right now, as it was to some of us even at the time these events were taking place, that President Obama was being prudent and sensible even while others were being viciously partisan, self-serving and greedy.  Over the long months of attempted negotiation and compromise, he gave in when he had to, for the sake of our national well-being and for the sake of averting national disaster, while he waited for enough people to realize at long last that none of his olive branches were ever going to be willingly grasped by the so-called "conservatives" who wanted to bring him down even if they brought America itself down into the rubble.

These unscrupulous manipulators have proven themselves not to be "conservatives" but "destructives" -- and this ought to be our new name for them. They have demonized the names "liberal" and "socialist." They have demonized anyone who still believes that through our elected government we can still do vital and efficacious things for one another, in other words for the common good of our country and all its citizens.

Right now, thanks to president Obama and to all of us who stuck with him, the Destructives and the Party of No are on the ropes. The rope-a-dope worked. They're half groggy and reeling and he is hitting them hard, making them pay for their cynical outmoded policies. And we all need to keep fighting on his side, going for the knockout in November 2012.

NOTE: Of course the Destructives bounced back, thanks partly to Vladimir Putin and the help he gave to Donald Trump that ended up putting Trump in the White House in spite of the fact that Hillary Clinton beat him by three-million popular votes.

# PART SEVEN

# THE CON MEN ARE COMING TO GET YOU

The entertainment business is full of liars, cheats, manipulators and con men of every stripe, and I have dealt with them for over fifty years, yet in spite of their efforts I am a survivor, still making movies and getting books published.

I have learned to (mostly) recognize these hucksters and snake-oil salesmen before they can rip me off too much.

And I recognized Donald Trump for what he was, almost as soon as I became aware of him.

The articles in this section give lessons that can be applied to any area of endeavor, including politics.

# CHAPTER TWENTY-EIGHT

## *The Con Men in My Own Life*

Part of the fun of the entertainment business, as well as the political business, is their atmosphere of hype, hoopla and hullaballoo.  None of us are immune to it. That's why Phineas T. Barnum said, "There's a sucker born every minute," which was the birth rate in the U.S. at that time.  The con job is harmless enough when all that's at stake is the price of a ticket to a side show that turns out not to be worth the money.  But when you're working at things that risk your own time, effort and livelihood, the hucksters, thieves and con men can really take you for a ride.

Sometimes the ride has its amusing aspects.  Other times there's nothing amusing about it at all.  At the end of it your hopes and dreams can be wrecked or derailed.

You don't have to be extraordinarily successful to be a target for the crooks. They'll latch onto you when you're on your way up, and try to turn your drives and motivations to their own ends.  As you start to make it, the flakes and oddballs continue to come around and so do the piranhas, anxious to sink their teeth into you and feed off of your efforts till your bones sink to the bottom of the pond.

If you think I'm exaggerating, then you're ripe to get taken.

Here are some of the weird, whacky, amusing, sometimes dangerous situations I've encountered in my own career:

## The Great Escape that Probably Didn't Happen

Before we made *Night of the Living Dead*, George Romero, Russ Streiner and I made several other attempts to get feature projects off the ground.  One day, while I was still in the army, an East German refugee named Aberhardt Rollick wandered into The Latent Image and expressed his burning desire to make himself famous on the Silver Screen.  He had already been on the TV talk show circuit, so he had "celebrity status" in George and Russ's  eyes, and our close friend Rudy Ricci ended up writing a script called *The Flower Girl*, depicting Aberhardt's escape from a Nazi concentration camp.

I was only involved tangentially in this project, through letters from Rudy and by taking part in casting sessions and so forth when I was home on leave.

We were never quite sure Aberhardt's escape from a concentration camp had ever actually happened.  Today, in retrospect, I'm fairly sure it had not. He claimed to have directed award-winning plays and movies in Germany,  but he had a neat "out" anytime anyone questioned his assertions about his past: according to him, all his personal records and documents had been burned by the Nazis.

I don't think the truth mattered to him when it came to making his way toward fame and riches in the "land of opportunity."  Using Latent Image's good name, he raised a pile of cash to make *The Flower Girl*.  Then he spent it all on rugs and furniture and a new car for himself.  He said that if he was going to be a movie director he had to look the part.  Not only did George, Russ and Rudy hate the fact that he had spent the money on himself, they  had never intended for him to be the director.  Rudy, who wanted to direct the movie himself, was so mad he almost tossed Aberhardt out of a fifteenth-story window. In a letter to me, Rudy said, "The money was there.  The equipment too.  I could see every frame, every character move, down to the blink of an eye.  But the German wanted to direct.  His ideas and mine were as different as sausages and elephants."

A few years later, Aberhardt did manage to make a really terrible film with another group of folks that he conned.  I remember a scene showing actors hanging by their thumbs from the rafters of a cell -- but their arms were bent and they were talking with no strain, so you could tell they must've been standing on boxes placed out of frame.

I used to run into Aberhardt Rollick from time to time over the years, and his appearance seemed to get shabbier and shabbier as his failure to "hit it big" etched itself deeper and deeper into his heavily seamed face and nervous, darting eyes.  The last time I saw him, he was running a hot dog shop.  I was walking to a garage where I had left my car for some repairs, and he was standing on the sidewalk there, and we chatted for a few minutes.  He had been in the news lately because a waitress had been raped and murdered behind the counter of his hot dog shop.

A few weeks later, I read that he was dead, too. He had been found in his car. A vacuum-cleaner hose had been hooked up to the exhaust pipe to pump carbon monoxide in through the window. We speculated that maybe his death was connected somehow to the murder of the waitress, but we never found out.

## The Merchant's Magical Disappearance

He was a rug merchant, so maybe he disappeared on a magic carpet. We never did find out for sure how he went, where he went, or why.

When he first materialized, he claimed he wanted to finance and produce a movie through The Latent Image. So George Romero dug out an old script he had written, entitled *The Whine of the Fawn,* and Rudy Ricci started revising it. The story was a good one, set in 15th-century England, about young people caught in the turmoil of religious wars and witch hunts. The entire project was cast and ready to lens, when the rug merchant walked away and never came back. His phone was disconnected. His place was empty. We couldn't even find him to ask what had happened. We heard rumors that he had suffered some sort of nervous breakdown and was institutionalized. We thought that maybe his extremely wealthy father had him put away to stop him from squandering a big chunk of money on a "nutty" movie venture.

## The Baker and the Hookers

One day around midnight, George Romero was working under heavy deadline pressure, editing a TV spot, when the buzzer rang.  He took the elevator down, unlocked the front door to our building, and was met by a five-foot-tall Nigerian named Godwin Akamigbo, who proceeded to tell a very sad story.  His visa was about to expire.  He was broke and starving, but he wanted to learn about making films and bring this wonderful technology back to Africa.  If The Latent Image could help him, he would see that money poured into our company from huge grants available through the Nigerian government.

George gave Godwin $300 and told him to come back tomorrow to talk some more with me and Russ Streiner.  His accent was so thick we could barely understand him.  He smelled awful.  He was wearing an orange canvas boat-shaped hat, a ruffled tuxedo shirt, a pair of tan chinos, shiny black patent-leather shoes, bright orange socks and a gray raincoat.  He was very handsome, with high cheekbones and exceedingly dark skin.  He seldom removed the orange hat or the gray raincoat, even though this was a very hot summer with temperatures running in the 90's.  Apparently he was used to even hotter weather in Africa, so in Pittsburgh he was always freezing.  He never changed his clothes, and I don't think he ever took a bath the whole time we knew him.

He told us he had come to America as part of a State Department program to assist Nigerians in learning modern trades and businesses.  In his country, he had been a baker, but he wanted to become a filmmaker now.  If we would take him on as an apprentice, it would be grounds for getting his visa extended.

Godwin knew next to nothing about film.  When he saw tail clips hanging in an editing bin, he would ask what they were and if they could be used for fertilizer.  Once he picked up a scotch-tape dispenser and asked me if it was a film magazine.  He thought the sticky tape hanging out of the dispenser was motion picture film.

We eventually learned that he had a wife and five children in Nigeria, but he didn't want to go back to them.  He said there was a civil war on, and if he returned he would be killed.  Of course we wondered: if that was the case, how was he going to help us set up a film bureau there?  How was he going to obtain government money?  He said he could do all this when the civil war was over.

One day he brought in a photo album to impress us.  It was loaded with pictures showing how the Nigerian delegation had treated themselves on State Department money.  They had been living like potentates in one of our most elegant hotels.  The photos showed them beaming, in fezzes and robes, reclining on plush pillows in the arms of a bevy of women who looked like hookers.  The album was like a glimpse into a harem.

Thus it dawned on us why Godwin Akamigbo had no desire to go back to his wife and five kids.  He had to learn about film or something -- anything that the State Department would approve of, so they wouldn't revoke his visa.  So they'd give him lots of money to spend, enabling him to live like a potentate once again, with his very own harem of American hookers.

Not long after we saw the photo album, we asked Godwin to depart from us. By that time, George had learned how to expertly mimic Godwin's accent and his queries about "fertilizer," and every once in a while, over the next couple of years, George would go into an impromptu "Godwin act" and made us howl with laughter.

However, I'm still not entirely convinced that the laughs were worth the couple of thousand bucks we blew.

## The Bomb that Killed New American Films

This is an actual bomb and an actual attempted murder that I'm talking about here, not just a joke or an attempt at a catchy subheading.

After Russ Streiner and I resigned from The Latent Image, we teamed with Rudy Ricci to try to raise money for two feature films, one written by me and the other by Rudy. We didn't want to form a permanent company, just a limited partnership to do the two movies. But, through a fellow we met at a party, we were led down the primrose path to our own destruction.

Let's call the guy at the party "Tom Flanagan." Tom owned a company that manufactured plastic doodads, and he said that the money to start the company was raised for him by "Peter Matz" and "Joseph Arbor" of "M&A Equity Corporation." M&A had raised $100,000 for Flanagan Plastics, which was now selling its doodads like crazy. Tom thought that Matz and Arbor could raise lots of money for us to make our films, but of course, he said, they'd want to "sit on our board of directors and keep a finger on the purse strings till you have a successful project or two and prove yourselves to them."

Flanagan set up a meeting with Matz and Arbor, and we showed them clips of *Night of the Living Dead* and some of the commercial films we had made, plus tons of publicity that had accrued to us by this time. They went bananas over our stuff and offered to raise $1,500,000 for us.  We would have to form a corporation though, and make it an ongoing corporation, not just a limited partnership, so it'd be attractive to long-term investors.

Russ, Rudy and I checked out M&A Equity with established people in the Pittsburgh business community, and all the references were glowing.  Many of the most respected financial institutions and businesses in town had money in M&A.  They all said that if we could get M&A to go to bat for us, we should jump at the chance.

So, we took their advice and felt pretty good about it.  We even stifled our own qualms about giving Matz and Arbor the right to sign checks from the account of New American Films, Inc., which was the name of our new company.  We started funneling free-lance jobs into New American to build up the bank account and make it look good for the upcoming stock issue.  We leased a lovely building for our headquarters, and borrowed $15,000 from one of our friends to pay for our prospectus, etc.

But no sooner did we deposit the $15,000 when it disappeared into the pockets of Peter Matz and Joseph Arbor. We confronted them on this, heatedly berated them in fact, but they said we were "making a mountain out of a molehill."  Arbor even said we were "being chicken-shit" to bring up a little matter of $15,000 when they were about to raise us a million and a half.

They wouldn't put back the $15,000. We took their names off of our signature cards at the bank, but we were locking the barn door after the horse was gone.  We still entertained vague hopes that maybe somehow the stock issue would sell, if the prospectus ever got printed.  I had to take over the writing of it, since we now had no money to pay the attorney.

We were about to meet with new lawyers to boot Matz and Arbor out of our company, when a bomb went off in Arbor's Cadillac.  The car was blown to bits in the parking lot of a chic restaurant. The man attempting to set the bomb blew his own arm off, and Joe Arbor wasn't hurt at all, since he was still in the restaurant when the thing went off.

Russ, Rudy and I came under suspicion for this attempted murder because we had a motive: the theft of the $15,000.  Presumably we were after revenge.  The FBI questioned us and our friends and business associates.  The Commonwealth of Pennsylvania refused to approve our prospectus, so we were unable to make any public stock offering.

Months later, the culprits behind the bomb plot were caught, convicted and sent to prison.  It turned out that some other people, besides us, who had been ripped off by Matz and Arbor, had tried to kill Arbor to collect on a $250,000 insurance policy.

By this time, New American Films was in a shambles. The Pennsylvania Securities Commission finally approved our prospectus after I convinced them that I had nothing to do with the bomb plot.  Meanwhile, all our wealthiest backers had run for the hills and we were unable to sell enough stock to launch the company the right way. We had one leg in the grave before we were even open for business.  We struggled for five years, trying to overcome the adversity, but eventually we had to fold the company.

## The "Political Whore" who Loved Chitlins

I guess they don't serve chitlins in the penitentiary.

That's why Warren James (not his right name) had such a strong craving for them.

He came to my office when the Democratic primary campaign was in full swing in the year that would see George McGovern nominated to run for president against Richard Nixon.  I was anxious to find a way to get some work in a national campaign, on behalf of the Democrats, and had already written letters to them touting the work Russ Streiner and I had done in state-wide elections for candidates including Albert Brewer in Alabama, Lenore Romney in Michigan and Governor Colon in Puerto Rico.  But so far I had not found an "in" to the right people who could arrange a pitch to the National Democratic Party.

Enter our "savior" -- Warren James, a tall handsome black man wearing a paisley dashiki, a full beard and an Afro.  He showed me a letter from Hubert Humphrey, thanking him for the work he had done mobilizing black voters in key primary states.  "I'm a political whore, that's what I am," said Warren.  "I make no bones about it.  I don't want to stick with Hubert.  I think George is gonna get the nomination.  But he needs somebody to help him land the black vote.  That's where we come in."

"Who's we?" I asked skeptically.

"Me and you.  You guys have the expertise and the sample reel.  I have the connection with McGovern's campaign manager.  I even have a script for a spot that's bound to sell him. We can produce the spot on spec, but it won't really be spec, 'cause I can guarantee McGovern's guy will eat it up once he sees it."

Warren showed me and Russ his script for the proposed spot, and we thought it was excellent.  It had an undertaker removing a tiny bundled-up body from the home of a black family. The narrator pointed out that the infant mortality rate among blacks was many times that of white children, and George McGovern with his keen awareness of social problems would address this concern when he got elected president.

I decided to go to Washington with Warren James to do some on-the-spot investigating and make sure he was all he was cracked up to be. While we were there, he got appointments with key figures on the McGovern campaign staff, and we presented our idea of doing a series of spots aimed at minority voters. The staffers encouraged us to produce our pilot spot.

Warren and I celebrated the night before we left Washington. He said it had been such a long time since he ate his mother's chitlins that he was ordering them every night at his hotel, which happened to be the Pitts Hotel, where most blacks stayed because even at this late date in the early seventies there was still a large degree of vestigial segregation. Warren said, "Their chitlins ain't as good as my mama's but I think you'll like 'em anyway," so I ordered a plate -- the first time I had ever tried them -- and found them to my liking. (Later, unfortunately, I was to find out why he had been away from his mama's cooking for so long.)

We had a meeting after Warren and I got back to Pittsburgh, and Russ and I agreed to foot the out-of-pocket costs to produce a pilot spot, if Warren James would line up the locations, do the casting and so on. He was an impressive and serious-looking man, so it was decided he would play the part of the undertaker. And we ended up making a commercial that was very effective -- in fact it was a real heartbreaker.

So far, so good.

But then we found out that Warren was borrowing money from the people in the black community who had donated the use of their homes, the funeral limousine, etc., and he wasn't paying any of it back.  Also, he was running up huge bills at hotels and restaurants and charging it all to us, and it amounted to several thousand dollars.  Needless to say, this was not part of our agreement with Warren.  And when we confronted him, he disappeared.  We were stuck with the bills, and we never sold anything to the McGovern campaign or any other campaign that year.

Some months later, an FBI agent came to see me.  He showed me a mug shot: a clean-shaven black man with a chipped incisor, wearing a prison uniform with an inmate number across his chest.  "Do you know this man?" the agent asked.

I studied the mug shot.  The name under it wasn't "Warren James."  It didn't look like Warren at first.  My mind had to add a full beard, an Afro and a capped front tooth. Then I knew for sure.  "He told us his name was Warren James," I said to the FBI agent.  "He has a beard now, and his tooth isn't chipped.  What do you want him for?"

"I'm not at liberty to say."

"Well," I said, "you're in luck because I have some film clips that show him the way he looks now.  I can give you the footage and you can have the frames blown up."

"That won't be necessary."

"Why not?  That mug shot you're using doesn't look much like him anymore."

"That's okay.  I was told to ask you if you know him.  I've done that.  My job here is over."

This was hard for me to fathom.  My idea of the FBI at that time was that they were lawmen of relentless determination and deadly thoroughness.  But such seemed not to be the case this time.

As it turned out, that was the last I ever heard of Warren James or whoever he was, and I don't know what all he was guilty of or if he was ever caught.

## Be on your Guard

If you're in the entertainment business, you have to realize that most people regard it as *fun*, but not exactly *serious*.  Therefore, in their eyes you are not quite a serious person.  If you were, you'd be in bricklaying, accounting lawyering, accounting or plumbing.  Money isn't a serious matter to you, art is.  Since con men believe that money isn't as important to you as it is to them, they don't feel guilty when they cheat you out of it.  To them, you're Just a starry-eyed artist.  What do you care about money?

But you're going to have to care about it if you want to make films, and if you want to build and maintain a career.  So watch out for the con men who are coming to get you!

# CHAPTER TWENTY-NINE

*Some Con Men are also Sleaze-balls*

I always treated actresses and models with respect and dignity, but there were always sleaze-balls who didn't, and I have had some run-ins with them.

One of my earliest examples of this happened in 1974 when my movie *The Booby Hatch*, a satire of the sex revolution, was released by Independent-International Pictures. Lo and behold, I got a phone call from a guy who said he was a film producer on location in Arizona, making a picture for Universal, and he was interested in casting some of the actresses who had been in my movies. He wanted to know how he could reach them immediately because the scenes they would be in were due to be shot the following week.

Adhering to my standard policy regarding such matters, I told him, "I'm not at liberty to divulge their addresses or phone numbers, but I will give them your name and number and have them phone you if they're interested."

He said, "I'm out in the Arizona desert and can't be reached very easily. This production is on the move a lot. I'd rather contact *them* whenever I can."

Well, I still refused to give him any information about the actresses, so he ended up giving me a phone number in Chicago where he said he could be reached within the next few days. I then phoned the actresses and told them, "This guy may be on the level, or he may be a creep. It's up to you how you handle him, but I'd advise you not to trust him too much and protect yourselves as much as possible."

I then phoned Sam Sherman, president of Independent-International and told him what had transpired.

"Oh-oh," Sam said. "I think I know who this guy is. Your movie must be playing in Chicago, let me check the schedule."

Sure enough, he was right. It had played in a multi-screen break the preceding weekend.

"This guy is no film producer, he's a sicko," Sam said. "Every time we have a sexy picture playing the Chicago circuit, he goes to see it, then he tries to con the actresses. I even wrote an article that was published in *Variety* last year, trying to warn everybody in the business about this nut."

So I phoned the actresses back and gave them this new info. One of them, it turned out, had already talked to the sicko. She said, "I *thought* something weird was going on. He asked me to send him color eight-by-tens of myself in all kinds of crazy costumes. He wanted me as a schoolgirl, an Indian maiden, a sorceress, and on and on and on, giving him a series of poses where I always ended up with my clothes off."

We both chuckled wryly but not happily.

I said, "You didn't give him your address or phone number, did you?"

She said, "I almost did.  But in the end I didn't."

"That's good," I told her.  "I'm glad I warned you. You always have to protect yourself.  There are too many nuts in this world."

Of course nowadays there is finally a Me Too Movement to deal with them.  But we have the Groper in Chief in the White House.  On the day after he got elected, I heard a news report about a nine-year-old boy who had groped a girl a couple years younger, in school.  And he defended himself by saying, "If the president can do it, so can I."

Donald Trump's moral leadership at work.

# CHAPTER THIRTY

*The Con Man in the White House*


The Founding Fathers were steeped in the humanities.

Donald Trump is steeped in his own tweets.

The Founding Fathers were deeply and intimately familiar with the poetry, philosophy and science of their day.

Donald Trump doesn't read much of anything.

The Founding Fathers enshrined moral and ethical considerations into our form of government, and they protected it with Freedom of the Press.

Donald Trump accuses writers, reporters and analysts of creating "fake news."

Yet he tells the most lies.  And many Americans are incapable of telling his lies from the truth, because they don't really know very much.

In an article in *Newsweek* in 1987, David Gates wrote:

"Three-fourths of high-school seniors don't know what Reconstruction was and can't identify Walt Whitman or Henry David Thoreau.  Two-thirds can't date the Civil War within 50 years.  Half are equally vague about World War I and don't know who Stalin or Churchill were.  And one-third think Columbus sailed for the New World sometime after 1750.

"These figures are scary for many reasons -- not the least of which is that high-school seniors are, at best, a year shy of voting age.  Scariest of all is the sheer darkness in all those unfurnished minds. Even television must be baffling: can young people who never heard of Reconstruction fully comprehend a cross-burning on the evening news or make sense of *Gone with the Wind* on the prime-time movie?  But frankly they don't give a damn. Unless *someone* does, civilization may perish simply because nobody bothered to pass it on."

In a survey of the audiences for the various TV news and information channels, those who religiously watched Fox News overwhelmingly believed that they were the best-informed viewers in America.  But when all the viewers of these types of channels were tested, the Fox News addicts proved beyond a doubt to be the *least* informed.  Fox News is Donald Trump's favorite channel.  He watches it for hours every day  from the White House.    And  he  has  many,  many  phone conversations with one of their greatest ratings stars, Sean Hannity, who seems to be his most trusted advisor -- never mind General Mattis, Secretary Haley, Secretary Pompeo or any of the other supposed experts on vital matters; three-quarters of the time they're all left out of the loop while Trump goes it alone, shooting from the hip and shooting his mouth off in ways that threaten national security, alarm our allies, and alienate the United States of America from the rest of the world.  It even seems that many of the president's rants, tweets and policy decisions are inspired by Hannity, who started his career by being a frequent call-in listener on Rush Limbaugh's program.

Limbaugh, like Trump, is full of unabashed braggadocio. He calls his string of hundreds of syndicated stations "the EIB Network." EIB pompously stands for "Excellence in Broadcasting."

Could it be that Trump copied his pompous, bullying, bombastic style partly from Limbaugh? They're both showmen who, like P.T. Barnum, keep on proving that "there's a sucker born every minute."

Trump's political capital depends on making millions of people believe in his simplistic non-solutions, such as:

Immigrants are all criminals of the worst kind.

Mexicans are rapists.

Muslims are terrorists. They all hate America and their goal is to destroy us.

Neo-Nazi groups and anti-Nazi demonstrators both have good people marching.

Vladimir Putin is a strong, effective leader, unlike Obama, who wire-tapped Trump Tower.

Kim Jong Un is a funny guy. He wants to do the right thing and get rid of nuclear weapons.

All women who accuse Donald Trump of groping them or abusing them sexually are liars.

Trump is bent on making us all believe that everything that comes out of his mouth, no matter how contradictory or nonsensical it may be, is the gospel truth, and everything else is "fake news." He's on a relentless and endless propaganda binge. His main goal is to poison the "jury pool," which is his base, forty million strong, who may riot in the streets if he gets impeached.

He already has their minds made  up not to trust the Mueller report  even  if Mueller's investigation turns  up damning evidence.  His true believers, the most fanatical ones, are much like him -- they don't read much, therefore their ability to think intuitively lacks depth. They are blind to nuance, and so they haven't seen through the charlatan instead of buying into him hook, line and sinker.

They might not deserve to be called "deplorable," but many of them are "low-information voters." They haven't learned the lessons of history because they don't *know* any history.  And a nation without knowledge of its past is like a person with amnesia.

To once again quote from David Gates' *Newsweek* article:  "One recent study of one-thousand 16- to 18-year olds found that over a quarter of them thought Franklin D. Roosevelt was president during the Vietnam War; ten percent said Peter Ustinov was a leader of the Russian Revolution."

This level of ignorance makes me fear that we may reelect Donald Trump even after he finishes exploding our national debt, wrecking our economy, and emasculating our Constitution.

# CHAPTER THIRTY-ONE

*Adolf Hitler's Trumped Up Glory Days*

Like Donald J. Trump, Adolf Hitler was given credit that he didn't totally deserve for tremendous advancements in Germany.  His propaganda machine made sure that he was praised for everything good that seemed to be happening and that his real or imaginary achievements were firmly cemented into the minds of the populace.

Today many people still wonder: How was Hitler able to rebuild Germany so quickly?  How was it possible for him to drastically reduce unemployment, control inflation, and advance technology in such a short time following the Great Depression and the depredations of World War One?

Well, according to an Internet posting by Harold Kingsberg, "the hyperinflation of the German papiermark ended in January of 1924.  During this time, Hitler was awaiting trial for his role in the November 1923 Beer Hall Putsch and hadn't yet written Mein Kampf...inflation of the German currency had been over for nine years when Hitler came to power.  He deserves no credit for ending it."

We can take note of the similarity between Hitler's

undeserved praise in financial matters and Trump's taking total credit for the boom in the stock market -- which was already underway and had tripled under the Obama Administration. Trump's tax cuts for already enormously wealthy corporations and our wealthiest Americans probably boosted the stock market even more, but how much is open to debate.

According to Mr. Kingsberg, "In 1929 the Great Depression hit and the German economy, which had been using bank loans from the U.S. to grow, took a massive hit, and few Germans had any faith that the Weimar government had any ability whatsoever to deal with the economic crisis...about three people in ten were looking for work."

This situation, once again, is similar to what President Obama faced in 2008 when he first took office. Our country was on the verge of economic collapse. Many so-called financial "experts," including Trump, thought that the automobile industry should be allowed to go under. But Obama didn't listen. He bailed out our auto makers. And now they are thriving.

Kingsberg goes on to point out that German public works such as the completion of the Autobahn were financed mostly through borrowing in the form of bonds. And another important source of income was privatization. In the wake of the Depression, many businesses had been nationalized, but now they were sold off to private interests. As I pointed out in a previous chapter, privatization of American endeavors is practically a mantra with Republicans.

Kingsberg: "The problem is that unemployment is

only one indicator of economic strength. Thanks to Hitler's directive to focus on rearmament, there were frequent shortages of food, consumer goods and even such raw materials as wood...he planned to deal with the shortages by plundering nations that he planned to conquer for anything of value...to keep people from complaining about the shortages, Hitler scapegoated various groups of people -- most notably the Jews and the Communists...he gutted countries and was able to absorb only 50% of their wealth, and he destroyed workers and enslaved them demonstrating that a slave worker produced only one-third of what a free German worker produced."

Kingsberg concludes by saying, "Good at building Germany is one thing...destroying others is another thing. Hitler was good at that."

According to Brandon Li in another Internet post, "Nazi Germany began massive deficit spending...they used this to build infrastructure and a massive military from scratch, creating the illusion that German had recovered when in fact it was only living on borrowed money."

Li goes on to say that if Germany were a person, he would not have been a rags to riches millionaire, he would have been an average middle-class person with maxed-out credit cards.

Doesn't this ring true of present-day America in many ways? Trump has milked the poor and the middle class in order to give massive tax cuts to the rich. He has created massive deficits and has put them on the backs of future generations. It's true that he hasn't put immigrants into concentration camps or gas chambers, as Hitler did, but he has demonized them and has separated parents from their children.

The greedy ones among us are causing the stock market to go up, perhaps a little more than it otherwise would have, because they are feasting on our financially poor carcasses.

Massive military spending under Trump has been financed, much in the same way that Hitler did it, by plundering social programs that benefit the poor and the less wealthy.  In addition, the ongoing wars started under George Bush continue to make armaments producers richer and richer even as they admittedly may help to reduce unemployment.

And Trump's bellicose rants and tweets help create a situation in which all Americans can fear the potential outbreak of even more foolish wars, a fear which in turn makes bloated military expenditures seem, to many, to be almost prudent.

The device of creating a massive threat in order to gain power and wealth or to maintain power and wealth has long been a favorite ploy of unscrupulous autocrats or would-be autocrats like Trump.  He quite openly admires so-called "strong men" like Kim Jong Un and Vladimir Putin.  If Adolf Hitler were alive today, Trump would probably invite him to the White House.

Adolf Hitler's trumped up glory days were the precursor to an ignominious downfall for him and for Germany.  Let's hope that the same fate does not await America.

# PART EIGHT

# WHAT WE SHOULD DO

There are two chapters plus an Afterword in this part of the book.  Chapter Thirty-One offers Sensible Solutions to some of the important problems that our society, our democracy, is facing right now, and Chapter Thirty-Two facetiously puts forward some Far-Out Solutions, food for thought that is also good for a laugh in some ways.

So let's get busy working together to *solve* our problems, instead of always being at each other's throats!

-- John Russo

CHAPTER THIRTY-TWO

*Sensible Solutions*

One of the biggest and most self-defeating problems that we have is that politicians need to raise millions of dollars to get elected or reelected.  As a result, their self-interest, many times if not *all* of the time, takes precedence over doing what is right for America.

## Term Limits

Therefore we should impose term limits.  I suggest that the president of the United States should continue to have a four-year term and be able to get reelected only once, for a total of eight possible years.  It was good enough for George Washington, who saw that he could easily have become a monarch, and he was wise enough and enough of a statesman to spare us that.  But it was only a custom for a long time, not a law.  Let's keep it on the books.

But in the case of our national legislators, let's make them equal with the president as far as the number of terms they can serve.  Let's equalize the House and the Senate, too.  Make them go into office or out of office in synch, so we can flush them all out at the same time if we want to.

In other words, make both them and the person they supported rise or fall on their joint decisions.

## Get the Money out of Politics

Congressmen spend more than three-quarters of their time raising millions of campaign dollars so they can keep on feeding at the public trough.  They won't be so bent on this if they have term limits.

But we also need public financing of elections, and we need to drastically shorten the length of campaigns, as is the case in England, for example.

We need to make them give full disclosure of where their campaign money comes from.  And we need to limit or even disallow certain contributions from certain sources, although this is a tricky issue because it may restrict freedom of speech.  Money talks.  But money has been talking too loudly for too long.

## Make it Compulsory to Disclose Tax Returns

For a presidential candidate to make public his tax returns has been a long-obeyed tradition, but Donald Trump brazenly and defiantly kept his hidden.  We never got to see who or what he was beholden to, financially.

He may be beholden to Russian money, or he may not be, and Robert Mueller's investigation may give us the answer.  But we should have been able to avoid all the damaging debate and intrigue and possible campaign violations.

We should also require candidates for Congress to disclose their tax returns, and for the same reasons.

And they all should be *absolutely required* to divest themselves of any businesses or financial dealings that could affect their critical decisions while in office. Trump is openly defying the Emoluments Clause of our Constitution, and his flunkies in Congress are letting him get away with it.

He is enriching himself and his family from the White House, and this needs to be stopped.

## Limit or Put a Stop to the Pardoning Power

It is absolutely ridiculous that in this corrupt day and age, or even in an age less corrupt, we allow the president a virtually unlimited power to pardon.

We should *absolutely forbid* him to pardon himself, and make this into a law that cannot be circumvented.

We claim that in a democracy nobody, even the president of the United States, is above the law, and yet we allow this vital principle to be muddied up and possibly used immorally and unethically.

## Reinstitute Laws that  Protect our Citizens

The EPA and consumer protections have been gutted under Donald Trump. He did these "dirty deeds" on the premise that he is a businessman who wants to "unchain" American companies who are too restricted by regulations. His spiel is that these regulations make it too hard for them to compete internationally.

What good is it if they can beat their competition while we are all choking to death from air pollution, as they are doing in China, or being poisoned by pesticides and polluted water?

As to our financial institutions, they already caused one disaster that almost collapsed the world wide economy during President Obama's tenure, and he handled the threat wisely and prevented the worst of it, and then laws were passed in an attempt to rein in the worst of the excesses.

Under Trump the protective regulations have been gutted, and they need to be put back in.

## Make College Education Free

When Bernie Sanders ran for president a key part of his platform was free education all the way through college and possibly beyond.

Why should our young people be saddled with debts so huge that they can't recover from them for decades, while they are trying to earn a living?

When the Founding Fathers revealed a Constitution that was giving the right to vote to "common people," the foreign monarchies laughed.  They said that the common people were too stupid to bear that responsibility.

But the Founding Fathers had a revolutionary idea, and they said, in effect, "That won't be a huge problem, because we are going to educate them."

Thus, we got free public education, and the results were enormously beneficial.  Education helped unleash the enormous energy, creativity and inventiveness of the "common people."  People like Thomas Edison, Henry Ford, the Wright Brothers, Jonas Salk, and on and on.

Free public education with a wisely constructed curriculum made people capable of understanding why and how their democracy works -- and works for the benefit of all our citizens.

By contrast, Donald Trump, even though he attended supposedly top schools, was able to avoid knowing much about our democratic system.  He was also able to avoid caring about it.  His Secretary of Education, Betsy De Voss, made a fortune owning private schools and destroying public ones.

She and Trump and others like them have a vested interest in the "dumbing of America."  The less people know about what is going on and why, the more easily they are manipulated.

Why do you think demagogues burn books?

Bernie Sanders' point is that a college education is the equivalent of a high-school education in our day and age.  In our highly advance technological and scientific society, our young people need higher education in order to compete and qualify for high-income jobs, so they won't be burger-flippers their entire lives.

In many, many ways, Trump and his minions want to keep the common people down.  That's why they love and keep on pushing fallacies like Trickle Down Economics.

That kind of "trickle" doesn't lift people up.  It enables those who already have money and power to keep on acquiring more, at the expense of all of us.

# CHAPTER THIRTY-THREE

*Far-out Solutions*

Sometimes I have wacky ideas, and some are wackier than others.  Some are meant to be taken a bit seriously, and some are mostly facetious even though they may contain several grains of truth.  In this chapter I talk about tongue-in-cheek fantasies like "reforming" Congress by means of a lottery, "improving" our schools by making them bigger and smaller at the same time, "purifying" elections by doing away with TV ads, and "enhancing" our judicial system by bringing back the stock-and-pillory.

I must confess that I don't find some of these ideas so far-out or farfetched.  In fact, several of them might actually work.  So, what do you think?  Give me some feedback, perhaps on my Face Book page.

## The Legislative Lottery

What if we selected one-third of every legislative body, state, local and national, by lottery?

To understand the wisdom of this, we have to understand what a representative democracy really is and how it came to be.

According to historians, Athens was the first real democracy, and as a city-state it was small enough to be virtually a *pure* democracy -- in other words, every citizen could vote on everything.  The Athenians were deeply concerned about the duties of citizenship.  According to historian Simon Goldhill, Athenian citizens were expected to attend the Assembly, to serve on the Council, to act as jurors, to vote, to take part in festivals, and to fight in the military.

What a difference that kind of attitude would make in our own system!

But of course modern cities, states and nations are much too large, complicated and unwieldy to allow every citizen to vote on everything.  So instead we have a representative democracy, not a pure democracy.  We elect people to represent us in city councils, state legislatures and the House and Senate.  They are supposed to always act in our best interests, but some people would say that lately they seldom or never do.

But what if they had watchdogs in their midst?

We select juries by lottery, so why not legislative bodies?  Or at least a portion of them?

To quote Goldhill again, "Nothing frightens modern democracies so much as the specter of popular participation."

Why are they frightened?  Don't they want anybody to see what they are doing up close?

I hereby suggest that we select up to one-third of our legislators by lottery, same as we select prospective jurors. I don't think that the common citizen would do a worse job than many of the scoundrels who spend millions of dollars to stay there and get rich.  In fact, un-beholden to wealthy benefactors, they might use their best judgment about what is good for *us* instead of what is good for *them.*

And I suggest that if the average person knew that he might actually serve in Congress someday, thanks to the legislative lottery, we would thereby have a great upsurge of interest, appreciation and understanding of the workings of our government -- and greater voter participation.

How wonderful it would be if everybody knew a friend, a family member or a guy down the street who was actually serving or had served in Congress!  The talk around the kitchen table or in bars, barber shops and beauty parlors might be elevated to a more vital level, instead of consisting mainly about baseball, hairstyles and local gossip.

Plus, the rapscallions who are already holding office would have a lot of watchdogs and whistle blowers looking over their shoulders.  How many of them would want to keep coming back, getting elected and reelected over and over again, if they were behaving dishonestly and scared of getting caught at it?

The effectiveness of my lottery idea could be bolstered by term limits for all.  If the legislators selected by lottery did a fine job and were deeply appreciated by their constituents, they could be reelected.  And if they legitimately made some kind of name for themselves by their wise deeds, they could run for some other office, even a higher office, so as to continue in politics.

We would end up with a better quality in our representatives and a finer, more astute quality in our citizens.

## Bigger and Smaller Schools

When kids went to school in their own neighborhoods, they were more subject to, and more comforted by, the effects of the old aphorism that "it takes a village to raise a child."

And they didn't have to be bussed every day.

Is there any way to keep kids in their neighborhoods for *much* of their schooling, and let them go outside of their own neighborhoods for *some* of it?

The biggest drawback to having smaller schools but many more of them is that we could not possibly afford to fully equip thousands of smaller schools with computers, physics labs, chemistry labs, gyms and gymnastic equipment, swimming pools, and on and on.

So, what if we kept the kids in small neighborhood schools for reading, writing and arithmetic, but then bussed them to much larger schools during part of the week or month?  Maybe somehow we could give them the best of all possible academic worlds.

Maybe some variation of this idea might actually work.

## How Television Corrupts Politics

One day it occurred to me, in a flash of insight or what some may call delusion, that television itself is at the root of the problem of too much money in our politics.  TV advertising is the main reason why it costs so much to get elected these days.

In Abraham Lincoln's day, a candidate could ride on

a horse from town to town, from village to village, and get up on a stump. But now there is little chance of getting elected unless you can reach millions of people on television. And this costs millions of dollars. Dollars that mostly must be provided by wealthy individuals and corporations.

Candidates and office holders must spend most of their time raising money instead of doing the people's business. They end up beholden to the millionaires and corporations who have backed them.

So, what if we severely regulated or downsized the amount of money that can be spent for political campaigns on television? Maybe we'd cut the problem off at its roots, like cutting off a drug supply by shooting the dealers instead of arresting the addicts. (Not that I'm advocating actually shooting the dealers, but you get my point.) I don't have any really definite or refined ideas of how to cleverly implement this strategy, but maybe a healthy debate over it would help clarify a modification.

## Bringing Back the Stock and Pillory

Largely due to the criminalization of drug use and the fanatical drive to put criminals in jail and keep them there through lengthy prison terms and mandatory sentencing, we have the largest criminal population per capita in the so-called civilized world. The poor and the persecuted among us no longer attach much stigma, if any, to anyone who has done prison time; in fact, in some communities it is actually a badge of respect.

So, what can we do to reform the situation?

Much as we lament the use of the stock and pillory in olden times, it did have one big advantage: stigma. Public embarrassment.  When you had your arms and legs clamped in those blocks of wood, you were at the mercy of anybody who passed by. They could pelt you with horse manure or rotten eggs, or they could presumably do much worse things to you, even things of a perverted sexual nature.

I can't think of anybody who would want to be locked in a stock and pillory.  But there are plenty of repeat offenders who don't seem to mind repetitive jail time.

Of course I'm joking about bringing back the stock and pillory.

I think.

But does anyone have a better idea?

Like decriminalizing pot, maybe?

# AFTERWORD

My urge to write about societal and cultural matters has a lot to do with the fact that the late Norman Mailer was one of my favorite authors. He did not confine himself to fiction even though his wonderful World War Two novel, *The Naked and the Dead*, catapulted him to fame when he was only 25. He went on to write many excellent novels and nonfictional books such as *Advertisements for Myself* and *The Armies of the Night*.

In fact, I got to thinking about the idea of downsizing our schools because of a similar suggestion made by Norman Mailer in *The Presidential Papers*, a book that he hoped President Kennedy might someday skim. But that probably never happened before Kennedy got killed.

Another of Mailer's suggestions was that, in addition to a Peace Corps, we should also have an Adventure Corps. He said that adventure should not be an opportunity only for the rich. Why shouldn't poor kids also have the chance of going on safari or helping to sail a schooner? The louts on street corners who puff themselves up and act like nasty bad-asses should get to prove to themselves whether they would chicken out or climb the rigging in a squall.

I finally got to meet Mailer at a fundraiser for the famous Pittsburgh medical examiner, Cyril Wecht, who helped Norman research his book on the death of Marilyn Monroe. A friend of mine let him know that I had read all of his books, so he wanted to talk with me, and when we shook hands the young lady he was with told him that *Night of the Living Dead* was one of her favorite movies, and so in that way he was primed to have a lengthy conversation with me, which I thoroughly enjoyed.

Norman Mailer was one of the most brilliant, insightful and flamboyant writers America has ever produced, and I do not claim to have matched his style and flair in this book.

But no one would ever sing if everybody had to be as good as Sinatra, and almost nobody would write if we all had to be as brilliant as Mailer.